C000200668

Some Herbaceous of the Saxifragaceae Family

Aileen Stocks

Front cover:
Darmera peltata (*Peltiphyllum peltatum*) and
Saxifraga × *urbium* (London pride) by Peter Bryan
two extremes of height in the range of plants covered in this booklet

© The Hardy Plant Society – November 1995
ISBN 0 901687 111

Acknowledgements

I would like to thank the following people for their help and support in providing information: Heather Booker (National *Rodgersia* Collection), Bob Brown (Cotswold Garden Flowers), Ted Brown (Ulverscroft Grange Nursery), Liz Bryan (for linguistic assistance), Peter Bryan (for art and design), Miss K. Budden (Glebe Garden Nursery), (John R.L. Carter (Rowden Gardens Nursery), Beth Chatto (The Beth Chatto Gardens Ltd), Dr Cullen and Gary Dunlop (for helping to clarify the plants in *Rodgersia*), Sally Grant and Gwen Grantham (art work), Chris Hallsworth (National Collection of *Bergenia*), Margaret Handley (Foliage & Unusual Plants Nursery), Judy Harry (Judy's Country Garden Nursery), Dan Heims (Terra Nova Nursery, USA), W.E.Th. Ingwersen (Birch Farm Nursery), Shirley-Anne Kennedy (art work), Sibylle Kreutzberger, Ron McBeath (Assistant Curator, Royal Botanic Garden Edinburgh), Henry Noblett (National Collection of *Astilbe*, The Lakeland Horticultural Society), George Parker, Malcolm Pharoah (head gardener of the National *Astilbe* Collection at Marwood, who revealed that when the Iron Curtain came down some long-lost astilbes were rescued from Latvia), Joyce Robinson, Jean Rush (art work), Joe Sharman (Monksilver Nursery), Elizabeth Strangman (Washfield Nursery), Baker Straw (Perhill Nurseries), R.D. Plants, Michael Wickenden (Cally Gardens) and Denis Dujardin from Belgium.

Astilbe 'Sprite'   **Peter Bryan**

Introduction

IN THE PRESENT TAXONOMIC UPHEAVAL, it is comforting to realise that one word, 'family', is constant and easily and immediately comprehensible to both amateur and professional alike. This booklet is concerned with a selection of members from the Saxifragaceae and it is hoped that it will reveal the wealth of plant material that can be found in this family.

The Saxifragaceae are a large family of approximately eighty genera. They are almost cosmopolitan though the majority are native to East Asia, the Himalaya and North America. Generally they are characterised by herbs with red root tips and basal rosettes of leaves. More particularly, they usually have four or five sepals, a similar number of petals (they are rarely absent as in rodgersias), twice as many stamens (occasionally fewer or more), two carpels and styles and capsule fruit (rarely berries). There are many species, ranging from tiny alpines to quite large herbaceous plants and, as their family name implies (from the Latin *saxum,* rock, and *fragere,* to break), they are mostly found in their native state on rock ledges and in crevices. Happily for the gardener, many of the more desirable varieties will thrive in quite a wide range of conditions.

One very important feature that they all share is the distinction of their leaves: often persistent throughout the year, the variation of colour, shape, texture and size of leaf is remarkable. Those of the bergenias are coarse and often red, totally different from the dainty fern-like quality of the astilbes or the ground-hugging saxifrages. Although some have insignificant flowers they do have a quiet charm when planted in drifts and the wide choice of colour invites inclusion in most schemes. The aim of this book is to provide a synopsis of those genera that can be classed as most suitable for use in an herbaceous situation rather than the alpine or rock garden.

Like all families, whether animal or plant, this one has the usual mixture of members. There are those that like to be cosseted and need a little extra protection; some that will thrive whatever the conditions; the slow and the rampant; the rare and the ubiquitous.

From the gardener's point of view, probably the greatest asset is the general good health of this family – there are no dastardly diseases or pernicious pests waiting to strike. Very occasionally some plants will succumb to rust and there will be times when some leaves will attract the attentions of lowly foragers but the majority will remain in the garden relatively unscathed.

Each genus described has an attendant minefield of taxonomy. While every effort has been made to be accurate, in practice this has been very difficult. Although classification is an exact science it is not a complete one and reference books and experts differ. Various reasons could account for this. Many of the cultivars were bred on continental Europe a long time ago and conditions elsewhere in cultivation might have resulted in changes in growth. Natural selection does inevitably happen, and also wrong naming or new names for old plants. Every day new methods and equipment reveal information that has been unknown or unavailable to our predecessors. If important or major mistakes can be rectified please inform the Collection holders or the Royal Horticultural Society.

The plants are listed in alphabetical order under their relevant species (where possible) as, obviously, they share the distinctive features of the species. This has saved much repetition of descriptions that are similar. There may be some discrepancies in the detailed descriptions too but one person's 'mauvy-pink' is another's 'rosy-lilac'. Also, there are bound to be different manifestations of the same variety given different habitats.

Whereas all the plants in this book can be grown and will be hardy somewhere in the UK, it is necessary to emphasise that temperature alone is not the decisive factor in determining hardiness: situation, soil, rainfall, drainage and other conditions have to be considered too. The USDA zones are used as an indication of hardiness:

Zone 3	-40 to -34 °C
Zone 4	-34 to -29 °C
Zone 5	-29 to -23 °C
Zone 6	-23 to -18 °C
Zone 7	-18 to -12 °C
Zone 8	-12 to -7 °C
Zone 9	-7 to -1 °C

The scheme is based on average annual minimum temperatures; the rating is based on open garden conditions. (The UK, for example, covers zones 6 to 9; only the Scillies are in Z10.) If a plant is rated Zone 8 it means it will usually survive a winter minimum of -7 °C, not that it will survive any winter in a Zone 8 area of the country – some winters may be unusually harsh.

Some of the plants covered in this booklet are registered and protected under Plant Breeders' Rights. Gardeners can propagate the plants for private and non-commercial purposes but the plants can only be offered for sale under license.

Most gardens will already contain one or more of the plants that follow, nevertheless it is possible that new friends will be made and maybe the answer to a 'problem' patch solved. The introduction is over; so now – meet the family.

Astilbe

THE NAME COMES FROM THE GREEK, meaning 'without shine', though accounts differ whether the reference was to the dullness of the leaves of the type species or the flowers. The first *Astilbe* to arrive in this country from China in the latter half of the nineteenth century was *Astilbe davidii* or, as it is sometimes classified, *Astilbe chinensis* var. *davidii*. Several more species from China and Japan followed and it was from these that the German nurseryman Georg Arends bred and selected in the early twentieth century to make his valuable contribution to the plants we have today.

Arends continued to propagate new cultivars until his death in 1951, even though his work was disrupted by two world wars, and his nursery is now continued by his granddaughter. At about the same time as Arends was raising his new cultivars, Lemoine, in France, was engaged in similar work, although few of his cultivars seem to have survived. Other plant breeders such as van Waveren and Kruyff in Holland and in more recent times Ruys (at what is now called the Moerheim Plantenwinkel), Theoboldt, Hesse/Weener, den Ouden (at the Friesland Staudengarten) and Pagels have been active, while in England the Bloom family of Bressingham has given us even more varieties from which to choose.

The original focus of Arends's breeding programme was on the pot plants so beloved by society at the time. Astilbes took quite kindly to this treatment, responding to 'forcing' in a controlled environment. Indeed, it is worth noting that if conditions in the garden are not naturally to their liking they will enjoy life in a large pot outside. The planting medium should be a rich, moist loam and it is essential that they do not dry out but the drainage is equally important (they should be moist but not soggy or waterlogged). Stand the pot in a saucer and it will simplify watering. On a north-facing site both the foliage and the flowers will provide a long period of interest throughout spring and summer and even in winter the 'rusty' desiccated spikes will persist for some time.

All the species bear a marked similarity in physical properties and habitat preference. The plants are small- to medium-sized in garden terms, ranging from 15cm (6in) to a possible 2m (7ft) in height and, being of a neat habit, need no staking. The colours of the flowers range from white to quite deep purple and every shade of pink and red in between. The foliage is ferny, with much-divided leaves and serrated leaflets. All are hardy and even if the foliage is damaged by late frosts they usually recover and the flowers are unaffected – racemes of tiny blooms rise above the leaves and will withstand quite adverse conditions.

In their native habitat in China, Japan, Korea and the Himalaya they favour the cool, moist, semi-shaded places near stream sides and where the soil is humus rich and well-drained. Hot dry conditions are anathema to them.

As garden subjects they can complement many a scheme. Many will naturalise happily in moist woodland. The shorter-growing varieties will enhance the front of the border and *Astilbe rivularis* var. *myriantha*, for instance, could make a dramatic statement as a specimen plant. Generally, their effect is stronger if planted in drifts or groups and although they will spread slowly they are not usually too invasive.

Propagation can be by division, preferably when completely dormant. *Astilbe chinensis* var. *pumila* can be increased by runners and stem cuttings. The species can be reproduced by seed in the autumn but it is not easy as it does not remain viable for much longer than three weeks. Once established the plants are best left undisturbed; if the roots become bare they can be covered with some good loam.

A. × *arendsii* Z4

These are hybrids involving *A. chinensis* var. *davidii*: with *A. astilboides* (flowers in loose panicles, stamens and petals are longer than the sepals); with *A.* × *rosea* (flowers are purple, pink to white); and with *A. thunbergii* (large nodding panicles to 1.75m/5½ft).

'Amethyst' G. Arends, 1930
Growing 80-100cm (32-40in) high, this has violet-purple flowers in early summer.

'Anita Pfeifer' G. Arends, 1930
Growing 55-60cm (22-24in) high, this has salmon pink flowers midseason.

'Augustleuchten'
See 'Paul Gaarder'. This is a sport of 'Else Schluck'.

'Bergkristall' ('Mountain Crystal') G. Arends, 1920
In midseason, the slender, white spikes grow over 1m (40in) tall.

'Brautschleier' AGM ('Bridal Veil') G. Arends, 1929
A good plant with snow-white, nodding plumes 60-90cm (24-36in) high in early summer.

'Bressingham Beauty' A. Bloom, 1969
The bright, salmon pink flowers appear midseason and grow to 1m (40in).

'Bronzelaub' K. Foerster, 1963
Growing to 50cm (20in), the light pink flowers appear midseason, shown off by the bronze foliage.

'Bumalda'
Possibly from America, the palest pink, almost white, flowers in early summer contrast with the dark foliage. It grows to 50cm (20in).

'Burgunderrot' Hesse, 1958
The crimson flowers appear in early summer.

'Catherine Deneuve' ('Bloast') A. Bloom, 1993
Named for the famous French actress. Growing 60cm (24in) high, the good, fluffy plumes of glowing rose pink, are borne for several weeks in the summer. It looks similar to 'Federsee'.

'Cattleya' G. Arends, 1953
An upright and vigorous plant, this grows to 80-100cm (32-40in). The rose to lilac-pink flowers appear in mid-to-late summer.

'Cattleya Dunkel' G. Arends
A red-flowered sport of the previous plant.

'Ceres' G. Arends, 1909
The pale lilac flowers grow to 90cm (36in) in midsummer.

'Diamant' ('Diamond') G. Arends, 1920
The white upright flowers, 80-90cm (30-36in) high, appear in early summer.

'Elizabeth Bloom' A. Bloom, 1989
Growing to 60cm (24in), this has dark green, glossy foliage and the purest pink, graceful but sturdy plumes for several weeks in late spring through to late summer.

'Else Shluck' G. Arends, 1930
Named for an employee of the Arends nursery, the carmine red flowers grow to 70-80cm (28-32in) midseason.

'Erika' G. Arends, 1940
In late spring to midsummer, this has clear, rose pink flowers, 60cm (24in) high.

'Fanal' AGM G. Arends, 1933
This is very popular. As the pomegranate-red flowers are early, it is good for forcing. Growing 60-80cm (24-30in) high, it has dark leaves.

'Fata Morgana' zur Linden, 1991
Growing to 50-60cm (20-24in) high, the crimson flowers appear in midsummer.

'Federsee' Theoboldt, 1939
The coral-rose to carmine-pink flowers form a dense spike 60cm (24in) high in midsummer. It will tolerate drier conditions than many others.

'Feuer' ('Fire', 'Cherry Ripe') G. Arends, 1940
A good, mid-to-late flowering plant, with carmine plumes 70cm (28in) high and light green foliage.

'Gertrud Brix' G. Arends, 1930
Named for an employee at the Arends nursery. Growing to 65cm (26in), the carmine-red flowers appear from midsummer onwards.

'Gloria' G. Arends, 1913
Growing 60-70cm (24-28in) high, the dark pink flowers appear in early summer.

'Gloria Alba' G. Arends, 1924
See 'Weisse Gloria'.

'Gloria Purpurea' Ruys, 1916
A good midseason plant with deep rose flowers about 60-90cm (24-36in) high.
'Glut' ('Glow') G. Arends, 1952
Growing 80-90cm (30-36in) high, it has rather late, bright red plumes and dark foliage.
'Granat' G. Arends, 1920★★
Suitable for the larger rock garden, growing 95-100cm (38-40in) tall, with bright red flowers.
'Grete Boucher' G. Arends, 1930
With red flowers in midsummer, it grows 50-60cm (20-24in) high.
'Grete Püngel' G. Arends, 1924
Named for an employee at the Arends nursery. The light pink plumes appear in early summer, growing to 50-60cm (20-24in).
'Harmony' Halls, 1975
This sport of 'Venus' is always much admired and quite distinct, with beautiful dark foliage all season and lilac-pink flowers.
'Hyazinth' ('Hyacinth') G. Arends, 1920
In midsummer, lilac flowers grow to 1m (40in).
'Irrlicht' Theoboldt, 1937
Blooms very early and has white flowers, tinged pink, about 70cm (28in) high.
'Kvele' ('Kwell') Nesaule, 1949
Growing about 90cm (36in) high, it has rose pink flowers in midsummer.
'Lachskönigin' ('Salmon Queen') G. Arends, 1910★
It grows to 1m (40in) and bears salmon pink flowers in midsummer.
'Lilli Goos' G. Arends, 1930
Named for an employee at the Arends nursery. The leaves are tinted brown or purple. It is late to flower with rose pink plumes, 70-90cm (28-36in) high.
'Mars' Verboem, 1927
1m (40in) high, it has dark foliage, and carmine flowers in midsummer.
'Martha Illing' Weinrich, 1978
Carmine flowers in midsummer; it grows to 90cm (36in).
'Öbergärtner Jürgens' Hesse, 1954
A selected sport of 'Fanal', the carmine-red flowers are early and it grows 65-70cm (26-28in) high.
'Opal' G. Arends, 1913
Growing 90cm (36in) high, it has light violet flowers in midsummer.
'Paul Gaarder' ('Augustleuchten') P. Gaarder
Growing to 65cm (26in), it has bright red flowers in midsummer.
'Rosa Perle' ('Pink Pearl') G. Arends, 1908★
Growing to 80cm (32in) or more, this has silvery-pink flowers.

'Rosenschleier' Spijker, 1973
This should be a pink 'Brautschleier' and is very rare. It grows to 80cm (32in).
'Rotlicht' ('Red Light') Pagels
Grows 60-80cm (24-32in) high and has bright red flowers midseason and dark foliage.
'Salmon Queen' G. Arends, 1910*
See 'Lachskönigin'.
'Snowdrift' Bloom, 1975
A dwarf plant growing to about 40-48cm (16-19in); the foliage is bright green and the flowers very white mid-to-late summer.
'Spartan'
Now considered to be the same sport as 'Rotlicht', it has dark red flowers midseason.
'Spinell' G. Arends, 1955
This blooms early with red flowers. It is a broad, bushy plant 80cm (32in) high.
'Tamarix' Ruys, 1917
A tall plant it needs constant moisture.
'Venus' G. Arends, 1910
A good, elegant plant, having soft, silvery-pink flowers in midsummer. 70cm (28in) high.
'Vesuvius' Verboem, 1940
Carmine-red flowers appear from midsummer onwards.
'Walküre' G. Arends, 1912
Growing 90cm (36in) high and with lilac flowers in midsummer.
'Weisse Gloria' ('White Gloria', 'Gloria Alba') G. Arends, 1924
Growing to 60cm (24in) or more, this early-summer flowering plant has pure white plumes and dark leaves.
'Weisse Perle' G. Arends, 1910*
Very like 'Rosa Perle' and 'Lachskönigin'.
'White Gloria'
See 'Weisse Gloria'
'White Queen'
This is possibly the same as 'Deutschland', growing 60cm (24in) high and having white flowers in summer.
'William Reeves' Prichard, 1930**
This is a sport of 'Granat', 90cm (36in) high, with dark crimson-scarlet flowers.

A. astilboides Z5
From Japan, this grows to 90cm (36in). The outspread panicles of dense, creamy-white spikes appear in midsummer. The leaves are pointed and hairy and it prefers moist shade. Not generally in cultivation; beware of selections of *A. japonica* offered under this name.

A. biternata Z6
Found growing in the Appalachian Mountains in North America, it has yellowish flowers in late spring-early summer and grows to 45cm (18in).

A. chinensis Z4
From China, this grows up to 1m (40in) high and bears slender, pyramidal, lilac-mauve flowers for several weeks in late summer to early autumn. It makes good groundcover; the *A. c.* types are generally more tolerant of adverse conditions.

'Finale' G. Arends, 1952
Late-flowering, with red-purple plumes held tightly over the foliage 60cm (24in) high.

'Frankentroll' Marx
From the Knöpnadel's nursery in Germany. Its flowers in midsummer are similar to the species in colour, a lilac-rose, and it grows 25cm (10in) high. It is not common in British nurseries but is popular with visitors to the National Collection at Marwood Hill Gardens. It spreads well.

***A. c.* 'Intermezzo'** G. Arends, 1957
Growing to 55cm (22in), it has purple flowers in late summer.

'Spätsommer' Weinreich, 1978
Growing to 75cm (30in), this has violet flowers in midsummer.

'Veronica Klose' H. Klose, 1983
A good plant with deep pink flowers in midsummer. 60cm (24in) high.

A. chinensis var. *davidii* Z4
Growing to 1-1.5m (3¼-5ft), the feathery, coarsely-toothed leaves are bronze-green when young turning darker with age. Small rose-purple flowers are borne on slender panicles in mid-to-late summer.

'Jo Ophorst' Ruys, 1916
This has a stiff, upright habit and bears purple-red flowers over 90cm (36in) high late in the season.

'König Albert' Ruys, 1916
Tall and white-flowered.

'Salland' Ruys, 1913
In good conditions this will grow 1.8m (6ft) high. The long, slender, erect spikes bear magenta-purple flowers in mid-to-late summer. The stems are dark and the leaves are dark green.

'Salland Purpurea'
Deep purple flowers in late summer

A. chinensis var. *pumila* AGM Z4
Short (35cm/14in), lilac-pink late flowers. A small plant with dense leaves it makes good groundcover and will thrive on heavier clay soils and tolerate some drought conditions.

'Serenade' G. Arends, 1954
This cultivar's feathery, pinkish-red flowers appear very late and it grows to 45cm (18in).

A. chinensis var. taquetii Z4
This is a late-flowering species reaching 1.2m (4ft), having dark leaves and reddish-purple blooms.
'Purple Glory' Ruys, 1985
A recent cultivar from Moerheim Plantenwinkel. It is the same height as the *taquetii* cultivars but the flowers are more pinkish than purple, flowering in midsummer.
'Purpurkerze' ('Purple Candle') Weinrich, 1978
Grows 75cm (30in) high and has violet-purple flowers in midsummer.
'Purpurlanze' ('Purple Lance') 1978
Growing to about 1m (40in) or more, this is upright in habit. The magenta-purple flowers are late and it is probably the last astilbe to bloom.
'Superba' AGM Vilmorin, 1916
Of narrow, dense habit and with shocking-mauve flowers in mid-to-late summer, this is a good plant and grows to 1.2m (4ft).

A. congesta Z6
This comes from Japan. It has bright green, ferny foliage, and creamy-white fading to buff flowers in late summer. Grows to 45cm (18in).

A. × crispa G. Arends Z6
A short plant with purple flowers and tight, crinkled foliage.
'Gnom' G. Arends, 1923
A compact grower with dark green foliage and pink plumes in late summer.
'Lilliput' G. Arends, 1927
Only growing 15cm (6in) high, it is suitable for the rock garden. The dark green foliage is stiff, and the flowers are purple-pink in midsummer.
'Perkeo' AGM G. Arends, 1930
As it only grows 15cm (6in) high, it is most suitable for a rock garden or the front of the border. The foliage is stiff and dark green and the flowers are dark pink in midsummer.
'Peter Pan'
Short with deep pink flowers in mid-to-late summer.
'Snow Queen'
This dwarf plant has stiff, glossy foliage and white flowers.

A. glaberrima (*A. japonica* var. *terrestris*, *A. glaberrima* f. *terrestris*) Z4
From Japan, this little-known species is suitable for the rock garden, with bright green, deeply cut leaves and 20cm (8in) high, pink panicles.
'Glenroy Elf'
From Ballalheannagh Gardens, this is a hybrid of 'Saxosa' (see below) and *A.* 'Sprite'. Tolerant of most conditions, it is a very good plant with feathery foliage, like a small 'Sprite' – hence the name, and pale

11

pink flowers, 15cm (6in) tall in early summer.
'Saxosa'
This prefers acid conditions and will give pale-pink and cream flowers in late summer. It is short, about 10cm (4in) high.

A. g. var. *saxatilis* AGM Z4
Suitable for the rock garden as it only grows to 20cm (8in). Abundant, erect, pink flowers in midsummer are accompanied by deeply cut, firm foliage.

A. g. saxosa
See 'Saxosa' above.

A. grandis Z4
From China, this species has large, divided leaves up to 2m (7ft) high and 1m (40in) flower panicles which are loose and yellowish-white in midsummer. It is an excellent plant for naturalising in semi-shade.

A. japonica Z4
From Japan, this species grows to about 40cm (16in), with sharply toothed, glossy, dark green leaves, and white flowers in the late spring.
'Amerika' ('America') Ruys, 1913
This grows 45-55cm (18-22in) high and has small, light pink spikes in early summer.
'Bonanza' Marx, 1978
The rose pink flowers appear in midsummer and grow to 50cm (20in).
'Bonn' G. Arends, 1930
It does better in moist soil and partial shade, the pink flowers appearing in midsummer and growing 45-48cm (18-19in) high.
'Deutschland' G. Arends, 1920
A good plant, having white, slightly scented flowers in late spring and early summer, which reach 40-50cm (16-20in) in height.
'Düsseldorf' G. Arends, 1936
The carmine plumes are borne 55cm (22in) high from mid-to-late summer.
'Emden' G. Arends, 1920
The violet-purple flowers, 45cm (18in) high, are borne in early summer.
'Etna' Ruys, 1936
Bright red flowers are borne 60cm (24in) high, from mid-to-late summer.
'Europa' G. Arends, 1930
This is very floriferous, having fluffy pink blooms 50cm (20in) high in early summer.
'Holsatia' Nonne & Hepker, 1937
60cm (24in) tall, the violet-purple flowers appear in midsummer.

'Koblenz' G. Arends, 1938

A compact plant, with rose pink flowers 50cm (20in) high in early summer.

'Köln' ('Cologne') G. Arends, 1930

Growing to 50cm (20in), it has violet-purple flowers from midsummer onwards.

'Lady Digby'

Possibly a synonym of 'Plumet Neigeux'. This has white flowers but is insignificant as regards garden use.

'Laura'

See 'Mevrouw Annie Van Lauren'.

'Mainz' G. Arends, 1952

The dark, purple-pink flowers appear midsummer onwards and it is about 50-60cm (20-24in) high.

'Mevrouw Annie Van Lauren' ('Laura') 1921

This is 55cm (22in) tall and has deep pink flowers in midsummer.

'Montgomery' Kooij, 1949

The dark red flowers appear midseason and it grows 60-70cm (24-28in) high.

'Möwe' ('Seagull') G. Arends, 1920

Reaching 50cm (20in), the rose pink flowers are in dense spikes in early summer.

'Plumet Neigeux' Lemoine

80cm (32in) high with pink-tinged, white flowers in midsummer.

'Queen of Holland' 1899

Grows 50cm (20in) high and has white flowers in early summer.

'Red Sentinel' den Ouden, 1947

Growing 60cm (24in) high with open spikes of crimson flowers in midsummer.

'Rheinland' AGM G. Arends, 1920

This is small at 45-48cm (16-19in) and has clear, carmine-pink flowers in early summer. The leaves are deep green and it will grow in sun or shade.

'Washington' van Waveren, 1899

Only growing 35cm (14in) high, this has white flowers in early summer.

'W.E. Gladstone' G. Arends

The white flowers appear from midsummer onwards.

A. koreana Z5

As the name implies from Korea. It is about 30cm (12in) high, with rough and hairy leaves and large flower panicles which are pink in bud but white in bloom in midsummer. It will tolerate drier conditions than many others.

A. microphylla
The slender, fine, dissected foliage grows over 1m (40in) high and the flowers are white.

A. m. pink form
As the species but with pink flowers.

A. m. var. saisuensis
According to the Royal Botanic Gardens, Edinburgh, the plant cultivated under this name is an *Aruncus*.

A. rivularis Z7
From the Himalaya, it can grow to 1.5m (5ft). The compound leaves are large and the loosely branched flowers white in mid-to-late summer. This species prefers moist to wet soil, preferably near water.

A. r. var. myriantha
As above but the flower spike is more branched and drooping. It is similar to *Aruncus* in appearance.

A. × rosea Z4
From *A. chinensis* and *A. japonica*, it resembles the latter but has pink flowers in summer.

'Avalanche' van Waveren & Kruyff, 1902
The large, dense, white spikes reach 60cm (24in) in midsummer.

'Drayton Glory'
See 'Peach Blossom'.

'Peach Blossom' ('Drayton Glory') van Waveren & Kruyff, 1902
The soft peachy-pink flowers can reach 60cm (24in) in early summer.

'Queen Alexandra' van Waveren & Kruyff, 1902
This has soft-pink flowers and was one of the first to be named by Georg Arends. This was one of the hardest plants to track down and the true plant may be lost.

A. rubra
From the Himalaya, it might not be entirely hardy in this country. It grows 60-100cm (24-40in) high and has crimson hairs and flowers in midsummer.

A. simplicifolia AGM Z5
This comes from Japan and only grows to 30cm (12in). The flower panicles are pyramidal and yellowish-white, appearing in midsummer. The true species is not common but the hybrids are good for cool shade, especially in the rock garden. They give red autumn foliage.

'Alba' G. Arends
This has the palest-pink flowers and is 20cm (8in) in height.

'Aphrodite' E. Pagels, 1958
Growing 35-40cm (14-16in) high, this hybrid has a weeping habit, dark bronze foliage and carmine flowers in summer.

'Atrorosea' G. Arends, 1934
Growing 40-50cm (16-20in) high, the short plumes of bright, dark pink flowers appear in midsummer. A hybrid.
'Bronce Elegans' AGM ('Bronze Elegance') G. Arends, 1956
A very beautiful, small plant, growing 30cm (12in) high. The clear pink flowers appear in late summer and are complemented by the good foliage.
'Carnea' G. Arends, 1923
Growing to 45cm (18in), the salmon pink, drooping flowers appear in midsummer.
'Dunkellachs' G. Arends, 1940
This plant has an upright habit, with rose pink flowers and coppery foliage. Reaching 30cm (12in), it is long flowering from midsummer.
'Elegans' G. Arends, 1927
Growing to 45cm (18in), its light pink flowers appear in midsummer.
'Hennie Graafland'
Of medium height, it has good, salmon pink flowers.
'Inshriach Pink' Drake
This plant is to be recommended, having dark, bronze-tinted foliage and 30cm (12in) high, fluffy pink plumes in late summer.
'Nana'
Growing 30cm (12in) high, it has light pink flowers in midsummer.
'Peter Barrow' Barrow, introd. Ingwersen
20cm (8in) high with pink flowers in midsummer.
'Pink Curtsy' A. Bloom, 1987
It grows 40cm (16in) high with salmon pink flowers in midsummer.
'Praecox Alba' G. Arends, 1954
40-50cm (16-20in) high with white flowers in midsummer.
'Rosea' G. Arends, 1918
It grows 40-50cm (16-20in) high and has dark pink flowers in midsummer.
'Sheila Haxton' A. Bloom, 1988
A *simplicifolia* hybrid with some *chinensis* var. *pumila* blood. Named for a propagator of perennials retiring after 30 years, it grows 30-40cm (12-16in) high, the deep pink flowers appearing in midsummer.
'Siska'
From Denmark, it grows to 25cm (10in) and has pink flowers in midsummer.
'Sprite' AGM A. Bloom, 1977
A *simplicifolia* hybrid with some *chinensis* var. *pumila* blood. A good plant with pale pink flowers in late summer lasting several weeks and dark green, deeply dissected bushy foliage. 40-50cm (16-20in) high.
'William Buchanan'
Short growing, only 20cm (8in) high, the cream-pink flowers are accompanied by crimson-tinted foliage.

A. s. × *glaberrima*
See 'Sprite'

A. thunbergii Z4
This originated in China and Japan. It is usually about 50cm (20in) high. The flowers, white or pink in mid-to-late summer, have a nodding habit.

'Betsy Cuperus' Ruys, 1917
In late summer, the long, elegant, weeping, pale pink spikes reach 1.2m (4ft) high. This plant does, however, need constant moisture.

'Moerheimii' Ruys, 1909
Growing to 90-100cm (36-40in), this has large leaves and white flowers in mid-to-late summer.

'Professor van der Wielen' Ruys, 1917
It grows up to 1m (40in) tall and will tolerate drier conditions. Arching sprays of white flowers in midsummer.

'Rot Straussenfeder'
Growing to 95cm (38in), this has red flowers in midsummer.

'Straussenfeder' AGM ('Ostrich Plume') G. Arends, 1952
This grows 80-100cm (32-40in) high, with coral pink flowers in midsummer.

A. t. var. fujisanensis
A small variety, from Honshu, Japan, closely related to *A. simplicifolia* but with trilobed foliage and very pale pink flowers to 30cm (12in).

A. sp. ex Yakushima
Pink and white forms of this unidentified dwarf species are grown.

HYBRID CULTIVARS

'Carminea' Lemoine, 1907
This grows to 70cm (28in) and carries deep pink flowers in midsummer

'Carmine King'
This is probably a previously established cultivar.

'Crimson Feather'
Beth Chatto describes this but with reservations as to its validity. It has narrow, slender spires of dark red flowers about 90cm (36in) high.

'Dagalet'
The origin of this elegant plant is uncertain; Piers Trehane considers it *Aruncus parvulus* 'Dagalet'. The creamy-white panicles of flowers reach 25-30cm (10-12in) high and the leaves are bronze in autumn.

'Ellie' A. Bloom, 1993
This was named for Alan Bloom's granddaughter. It has fresh green

foliage and clear creamy flowers, 60-70cm (24-28in) high, which last for several weeks from late spring to late summer.

'Magenta' Lemoine, 1910
Growing 90-100cm (36-40in) high, it has violet flowers in midsummer.

'Mont Blanc' Lemoine, 1914
The white flowers appear in midsummer and it grows 70-80cm (28-32in) high.

'Örestad'
Possibly a *japonica* hybrid, this has dark pinkish-red flowers and grows 60cm (24in) high. It is available in Germany but not yet here. It is not particularly special.

'Red Admiral'
Possibly an incorrect name; it could be a synonym of 'Red Sentinel'. The bright green leaves have red stems, as do the bright dark wine coloured flowers which appear in early summer. Compact plant growing to 37cm (15in). Tolerates dryish conditions.

'Robinson's Pink'
Possibly *A.* × *rosea* 'Peach Blossom'.

'Solferino' Lemoine, 1910
Growing 80-100cm (32-40in) high, the lavender-pink flowers appear in midsummer.

sp. CLD 1559
Collected on Kew, Edinburgh and RHS expedition to the Yunnan province of China in 1990. 1.5m (5ft) high, with fresh green leaves and large white flowers drooping at the tip in late summer.

* According to Dr J.A. Smart, there seems to be some confusion regarding the three Arends cultivars 'Rosa Perle', 'Weisse Perle' and 'Lachskönigin' ('Salmon Queen'). Further work needs to be done in identifying them accurately.
** There is some confusion between the cultivar 'Granat' and its sport 'William Reeves'.

Astilboides tabularis **leaves, see overleaf**   **Jean Rush**

Astilboides

T HE NAME COMES FROM THE GREEK, meaning 'like an astilbe'. The genus is a native of the northern provinces of China.

Astilboides tabularis (*Rodgersia tabularis*) Z5
A native of north-east China and North Korea, this plant has similar peltate leaves to *Darmera* but paler and smoother, up to 90cm (36in) across. The flowers are like astilbe's in a plume up to 1.5m (5ft) in late spring to midsummer.

Bensoniella

N AMED FOR G.T. BENSON (1896-1928), author, the plant comes from north-west California and south-west Oregon.

Bensoniella oregona Z6
This has low clumps of rounded green leaves and produces short spikes of fluffy, cream-coloured flowers 20cm (8in) high in late spring. It is a rare plant and closely allied to *Mitella*, though it has lighter green leaves and is less tolerant of sun. It prefers woodland soil in part shade.

Bergenia

T HE NAME OF THIS GENUS commemorates Karl August von Bergen (1704-60), professor at Frankfurt.
  These are strong-growing, robust perennials from eastern Asia with creeping rhizomes which soon form large clumps. Some, like *Bergenia cordifolia*, have been with us since the seventeenth century and have long proved their worth. In the late-nineteenth century William Robinson described them with obvious approval. He mentions one of the first selections, a seedling from *B. cordifolia* called 'Purpurea', as a noble plant. It still gives pleasure today. No doubt there are people who will remember these plants by the name 'megasea' but, whatever their title,

they have been decorating the garden for many a century and have seldom found disfavour.

Bergenias provide good material for plant breeders and their work has produced some lovely additions for the garden. William Robinson also spoke well of a series of hybrid megaseas produced by Mr T. Smith of Newry, the result of crosses between *B. cordifolia* and *B. purpurascens*. 'Splendens' 'Brilliant', 'Campana' and 'Corrugata' were some of these. Sadly, the last two are no longer mentioned today but they may still survive in old gardens or under new names. Arends, Klose and, more recently, Hallsworth have all made valuable contributions; Eric Smith's hybrids with the names of composers are all well-known.

All the plants mentioned in the following pages are hardy in the UK and all have a similar form of growth, leaf structure and flower formation with only minor variations in colour and size.

The familiar leathery leaves, being evergreen, contribute to the structure of the garden all through the year and can be used to great advantage in many areas. As groundcover the wide variety of leaf colour available will complement many other plants. I have seen a narrow north-facing border fringed with bergenias, interplanted with spring bulbs and backed by Japanese anemones which has looked good all the year with very little maintenance. It is worth noting that a good feature can be created, especially for the winter, by growing them in containers on the patio. This is not a new fashion, for a hundred years ago William Robinson described *B. milesii* as being dwarf, nearly deciduous and a distinct and beautiful plant, especially if grown in pots in a cold house or sunny frame. Bergenias will be happy in light shade mixed with shrubs or ferns but will not thrive in water-logged ground or excessive drought or heat.

Bergenia species may be propagated by seed and will flower after two or three years. The seed is very fine (4,000 seeds weigh about 1g) and when sown it should not be covered but pressed gently and firmly on the surface of the compost and germinated at a temperature of 20 °C (68 °F). Rhizome cuttings can be taken mid-autumn to early spring.

Bergenias do not usually suffer from pests or diseases, apart from the dreaded vine weevil, and care should be taken when planted in pots. They can shelter slugs and snails under their leaves.

B. acanthifolia hort.
See *B.* × *spathulata*

B. beesiana Z4
See *B. purpurascens*

B. ciliata Z5
A native of Afghanistan and south-east Tibet, it has white to pale pink flowers which deepen in colour with age. They grow to 15-25cm (6-10in)

from spring to midsummer. The leaves are large, round, bright green and hairy on both sides. They reach 30cm (12in) across and colour red in the autumn.

It is considered a collector's plant and is probably the most difficult to grow. The plant prefers cool shade but flowers and new leaves are sensitive to late frosts so it needs a sheltered spot or protection – as does *B. ciliata* f. *ligulata,* sometimes listed as a separate species in catalogues.

B. c. forma *ligulata* Yeo (Wallich), 1966
Being early, the dense heads of nearly-white flowers with their contrasting red calyces need protection in late winter. These emerge before the hairy-margined leaves, which are broad and rounded.

B. c. 'Patricia Furness'
The leaves are hairless and 15cm (6in) across. It has a dense white flower with pink stamens and calyx.

B. cordifolia Z3
This native of Siberia was a favourite of Gertrude Jekyll. It flowers in late winter and early spring and the individual purplish-pink blooms can be 2.2cm (1in) in diameter. The leaves are hairless, leathery and remain green in winter. Old and reliable (it has been grown since the seventeenth century), it forms large clumps and is tolerant of cold and heat.

B. c. 'Purpurea' AGM
Spectacular foliage: the large, round leaves turning purple in the winter. Magenta flowers 60cm (24in) tall.

'Redstart'
Very attractive deep-red-margined leaves in winter and strong-red flowers. It is a good 'grower'.

'Rosea'
This has large, rounded, crinkled leaves and stumpy, rose pink blooms held close to the foliage.

B. crassifolia Z3
This native of Siberia and north-west China is outstanding. The bright purplish-pink flowers grow up to 30cm (12in) high in early spring with a drooping habit and the leaves turn a reddish-brown in the winter.

B. c. 'Autumn Red'
This is a good vigorous groundcover plant with flowers up to 75cm (30in) high.

'Croesus'
This is more suited to the rock garden, being dwarf and compact with bright pink flowers.

B. c. DF90028
Collected by Derek Fox from the Lake Baykal region of the former USSR. The nodding clusters of rose-purple flowers can reach 45cm (18in) high in spring. It has large leathery ovate leaves and will tolerate any soil in sun or shade.

B. c. var. *pacifica* Z4

This variety, also from Siberia, is less vigorous and possibly blooms a little later than the species. The leaves are slightly wider and the petals slightly longer with a more intense rose-purple colour with a reddish tint.

Bergenia cordifolia leaves   Shirley-Anne Kennedy

B. *hissarica*

Unknown in the UK, it is very similar to *B. stracheyi*, with whitish rose-coloured flowers.

B. × *media* Z3

A hybrid of *B. cordifolia* and *B. crassifolia*, it is reported to resemble *B. crassifolia*. The plants are often dwarf in stature with leaves broadly ovate at the base. It flowers in late winter and spring.

B. *milesii*

Possibly a synonym or a variant of *B. stracheyi*.

B. *purpurascens* AGM (*B. beesiana*) Z3

A native of Afghanistan through the Himalaya to south-west China. It is a good plant for winter when the narrow, vertical leaves turn a deep crimson. The flowers in late winter and spring are dense and a deep pink-purple on tall stalks up to 30cm (12in) high. It has a less spreading habit than many other bergenias.

B. p. var. *delavayi*
This is from the north-west Yunnan and has nodding clusters of pink flowers in the spring up to 30cm (12in) high. The shallowly denticulate leaves are leathery and dark green.

B. × schmidtii AGM (*B. crassifolia* 'Orbicularis', 'Speciosa') Z4
A hybrid of *B. ciliata* and *B. crassifolia,* it is vigorous and, often the first to flower, is frequently damaged by frost. Green leaves turning reddish in winter. It forms a mound 15cm (6in) high and the long-stalked, almost perfectly round red flowers (to 30cm/12in) are useful for indoor arrangements.

This is the most vigorous and most widely cultivated of the bergenias and is recognised by the ciliate edge to the leaves. The typical clone is called 'Ernst Schmidt'.

B. × smithii Z3
A hybrid of *B. cordifolia* and *B. purpurascens,* it is rare in cultivation. The late flowers are a pink to reddish-purple. There is no winter change in leaf colour.

'Brilliant'
Several different ones are offered under this name, some with large leaves and some with small. The original true cultivar is possibly lost. The flowers are drooping, a deep-purple, paling with age.

'Cascade'
The lilac flowers (darker on the back) are borne on long stems and the leaves are coarse.

'Distinction' T. Smith, 1889
The short-stalked, pale green, bullate leaves form distinct rosettes and although the attractive clear-pink flowers are individually small they form large heads on tall stems.

'Profusion' T. Smith, *c.* 1880
Similar to *B. cordifolia* with pale pink flowers.

'Progress' T. Smith, 1889
Raised in Ireland, it is similar to its parent though the flowers are non-drooping. The abundant carmine-red flowers are late. The leaves are green in winter.

B. × spathulata (*B. acanthifolia, B. ciliata* × *B. stracheyi*) Z5
Its origins are somewhat obscure. Chris Hallsworth, National Collection holder, explains: 'The name *B. acanthifolia* originates from a plant cultivated at Cambridge Botanic Garden (herbarium specimens from there can be seen dated March 1960 and March 1961). The plant was

previously cultivated at the Royal Botanic Garden, Edinburgh. It is not a valid name: *B.* × *spathulata* dated from an herbarium specimen of 1928 or a specimen of unknown origin in Belgium dated 1926 which superseded the Cambridge naming.'

This is a hybrid species of *B. ciliata* and *B. stracheyi*, the largest and the smallest-leaved species in the genus. The leaves are small, hairy and a light green with toothed edges, making a mound 15cm (6in) high. This is not always evergreen and severe frost may destroy all the foliage. The pale pink flowers, 20-30cm (8-12in) high in spring, darken with age.

B. sp. Mrs Crawford
Collected by Mrs Crawford in Kashmir and named after her by Beth Chatto, it has not been determined which species it belongs to. Markedly different from any other, it has compact clusters of leaves turning brilliant red and yellow in autumn and winter. The flowers are pure white.

B. stracheyi Z4-Z9 (depending on provenance)
This is a native of Afghanistan and northern India. This species and its white cultivar, 'Alba', were the parents of Eric Smith's hybrids. These all have evergreen leaves, some turning purple and red in the winter. It flowers in early spring with loose, pink, drooping clusters and it is particularly suitable for edging. Growing to 30cm (12in), it is sometimes damaged by late frosts.

B. s. 'Afghanica'
This is similar to 'Alba' having hairy, less shiny leaves.

B. s. 'Alba'
Compact, with clear, white blooms held like drumsticks, this is a useful plant, even if slightly tender. The leaves are dark green and it is about 15cm (6in) high.

B. spp. KBE 151 and KBE 209
Each is distinct and was collected during the 1983 Kashmir Botanical Expedition by Chadwell, Howard, Powell and Wright. Both of these plants have been grown by Chris Hallsworth from this seed but they did not appear to be good garden plants and were not very hardy. Possibly of *B. stracheyi* origin.

HYBRID CULTIVARS

'Abendglocken' ('Evening Bells') G. Arends, 1971
It has reddish-green leaves and dark reddish-pink flowers in the spring. 40cm (16in) high.

'Abendglut' ('Evening Glow') G. Arends, 1950
It dark red, semi-double flowers growing to 25-30cm (10-12in) in the spring and bronze-brown leaves with crinkled edges in the autumn.

'Admiral' R. Eskuche
The small, loose, red-pink flowers grow 30cm (12in) high in the spring.
The handsome, dark green leaves turn red in the winter.

'Apple Court White' R. Grounds, *c.* 1978
A green-eyed, white-flowered plant, it appeared in a cottage garden as
a lone white spike among all-pink bergenias. It is similar to *B. cordifolia*,
though the leaves are larger, and grows to approximately 38cm (15in).

'Baby Doll' zur Linden
This hybrid cultivar has pale pink flowers, which darken several shades
with age and are held 30cm (12in) high above green leaves in the spring.

'Bach' E. Smith, *c.* 1972
One of Eric Smith's hybrids which were named after composers, this
has pale pink flowers and bronze leaves.

'Ballawley' ('Delbees') pre-1950
Both the flowers and their stalks of this hybrid cultivar are bright red in
the spring. The leaves are green, large and flabby and up to 20cm (8in)
across; they turn bronze in the winter. Although growing to 60cm (24in)
high it is not very free-flowering and is best given some protection.
Raised at Ballawley Park, near Dublin, this name refers only to plants
vegetatively propagated from the original clone. Seed-raised plants,
which may differ considerably, should be called Ballawley Hybrids.

'Ballawley Guardsman'
A good selection from the Ballawley Hybrids (according to the National
Collection holder) which has improved flowers and winter leaf colour,
quite distinct from ordinary Ballawley stock.

'Bartók' E. Smith, early 1970s
One of the hybrids named after composers, a Ballawley Hybrid. It is
slow to increase but a superb plant for the winter, its leaves being large
and crinkled and turning a glowing bronze. It is vigorous and will reach
60cm (24in) in height.

'Beethoven' E. Smith, *c.* 1972
One of the hybrids named after composers, the dark green leaves have
red stems and the flowers are white with red calyces.

'Bizet' J. Archibald, *c.* 1976
One of the hybrids named after composers, similar to 'Ballawley' but
more compact. The carmine-red flowers and stems grow to 75cm (30in)
and it gives good winter colour.

'Borodin' J. Archibald, *c.* 1980
One of the hybrids named after composers. Similar to 'Bartók', a
Ballawley Hybrid, this cultivar is slightly smaller at 50cm (20in) but it
makes a large plant. The carmine flowers are in large bunches and the

leaves are impressive.

'Brahms' E. Smith, *c.* 1972
One of the hybrids named after composers, this has pale pink loose flowers and green leaves.

'Bressingham Bountiful' Pugsley, 1972; introd. A. Bloom
The branched flowers of this cultivar are a rosy-pink. The leaves are dark and sometimes damaged by frost.

'Bressingham Ruby' A. Bloom, 1982
This cultivar is a very hardy plant with a compact habit and abundant rose red flower spikes. With glossy green leaves turning maroon and ruby-red undersides, this is an outstanding plant in winter; A. Bloom described it as having the most colourful leaves he had ever seen in a bergenia.

'Bressingham Salmon' A. Bloom, mid-1970s
In spring this hybrid cultivar has distinctive salmon pink flowers 25cm (10in) high.

'Bressingham White' AGM A. Bloom, mid-1970s
With good freedom of flower and leaf this cultivar is a robust plant and better than most other whites.

'Britten' Introd. J. Archibald, *c.* 1977
This has pale pink flowers with red stems and small, coloured leaves.

'Clare Maxine'
This cultivar has a fabulous winter leaf colour, with large, shiny, bronze foliage and carmine-red flowers.

'Christopher Hallsworth' ('Variegata') C. Hallsworth
A variegated-leaved plant bred from a cross with 'Pugsley Pink', it is compact and very unusual. The second generation raised from seed came true with white, cream, pink and red leaf markings. The flowers are carmine.

'Elite'
This compact cultivar is often damaged by frost but does have bronze leaves in the winter and free-flowering blooms of deep rose red held high.

'Eric Smith'
Eric Smith gave this plant to Beth Chatto when he left Hadspen House and she regards it as possibly the best of all bergenias for winter effect. The leaves are large, round and wavy-edged with brilliant plum and crimson colouring.

'Evening Glow'
See 'Abendglut'.

'Flore Pleno'
A good dwarf variety. This rare cultivar has semi-double, deep pink flowers; flowers can be double or single ar different times. The older leaves turn red in the autumn. It is about 15cm (6in) high.

'Glockenturm' ('Bell Tower') R. Eskuche
This is very floriferous, with red-pink flowers to 30cm (12in) in spring.

'Helen's Bay' (*B. spathulata* 'Gambol')
This originated in a west coast of Ireland garden and is sometimes damaged by winter cold and wet. Compact in habit it has large round bunches of white flowers.

'Illusion' H. Klose, 1983
Although this cultivar has no red winter leaf colour, the flower stems are red. It often produces semi-double blooms with long pink petals and deep rose sepals.

'Jo Watanabe'
Named by Beth Chatto for Jo Watanabe from whose garden it came. The narrow, tongue-shaped leaves of this cultivar colour well and it has bright pink flowers in the spring.

'Margery Fish' ('Lambrook') H.C. Pugsley
A cross between *B.* 'Ballawley' and *B. ciliata*, it was named in honour of one who loved bergenias. It grows to 45cm (10in), the deep rose-red flowers appearing early spring. The large, bright green leaves are tinted red in the autumn.

'Minima'
Possibly a synonym to *B. cordifolia minor*. This poor cultivar is not gardenworthy; a compact plant, a shy bloomer with small, lilac-pink flowers and no winter colour.

'Morgenröte' AGM ('Morning Red', 'Dawn', 'Morning Blush') G. Arends, 1950
The bright pink flowers, 20-30cm (8-12in) high, can recur until autumn if the weather is cool. The leaves are small, crinkled and deep green.

'Öschberg'
This cultivar is very tall, reaching 50-60cm (20-24in). The bright pink flowers are late and so it is good in areas with late frosts. The leaves colour red in the winter.

'Opal'
Handsome shell pink flowers but not especially good winter colour.

'Perfect'
The carmine-red flowers have a drooping habit; about 25-30cm (10-12in) high, with small leaves.

'Pinneberg' Kikillus
Erect in habit with carmine-red flowers, the leaves of this hybrid cultivar colour red in the autumn.

'Pugsley's Pink' H.C. Pugsley
It has good pink flowers and red undersides to the leaves. Grows 35-50cm (14-20in) high.

'Pugsley's Purple' H.C. Pugsley
This cultivar is vigorous but not very free-flowering. The carmine to magenta blooms are late and strong.

'Purpurglocken' ('Purple Bells') G. Arends, 1971
40cm (16in) high, with dark green leaves and purple-red bell flowers which rebloom in the autumn.

'Purpurkönig' ('Purple King')
A small plant with little root growth. The flowers are short and pink to red in colour.

'Rathekim'
A good groundcover cultivar with coarse leaves, shy flowering with short lilac-pink blooms.

'Rosette' Bornim
A splendid plant with probably the largest flowers in the genus. The shell pink blooms are held well clear of the large leaves.

'Rosi Klose' H. Klose, 1982
About 30cm (12in) high, it has light salmon pink flowers.

'Rotblum'
Reaching 60cm (24in) high, this cultivar gives good autumn colour and pink flowers in the spring.

'Schneekissen' ('Snow Cushion', 'Schneekönigin') K. Foerster
A very tall plant up to 50cm (20in) high with slow, compact growth. The white, very pale-pink tinted flowers are good for cutting. It blooms early to midseason.

'Schneekönigin' ('Snow Queen') K. Foerster
See 'Schneekissen'.

'Silberlicht' AGM ('Silver Light') G. Arends, 1950
This is a good, strong, vigorous grower with large leaves and white flowers in the spring which turn pink.

Snowblush Hybrids E. Smith & J. Archibald, c. 1975
These compact plants have some winter leaf colour. The flowers are white with variable pink markings to some petals, fading to pink. Attractive and popular bergenias.

'Sunningdale' G.S. Thomas, 1964
A good groundcover plant with carmine to lilac flowers and magenta leaf colour in winter. It will tolerate full sun.

'Sunshade' Introd. Barr & Sons, 1902
This forms close rosettes, exaggerated by short leaf petioles. The blooms have narrow, drooping flowers of deep purple with reddish sepals in spring.

'Traum' H. Klose, 1983
It is not vigorous and may be tender. The bright pink flowers are held well clear of the foliage.

'Tubby Andrews' 1993
Variegated cream, yellow and green leaves; the spashed marks are variable and unstable. It is not a vigorous plant. Blooms mid-to-late season with carmine-purple flowers.

'Vorfrühling' H. Klose, 1977
This is unusual: the leaves are typical but the flower stalk is thick and tall. Characteristic are the stigmas, which are green and very prominent. The flowers are small and the petals only protrude slightly from the reddish calyces.

'Walter Kienli'
A tall-flowering cultivar with beautiful, large, wavy-edged leaves. It is, however, a late, shy, bloomer with tightly compressed heads of lilac-pink blooms fading to carmine.

'Wintermärchen' ('Winter Fairy Tale')
A durable plant, with narrow, leathery leaves turning red in winter. It is frost tolerant and the late, carmine-pink flowers are 30-40cm (12-16in) high.

'Winterzauber'
The winter leaf colour is very deep, almost a 'kidney' red.

Boykinia

THE NAME COMMEMORATES the field botanist Dr Samuel Boykin (1786-1846) of Georgia, USA. Found mostly in the wild in western North America, the principal use of this group is where extensive areas of groundcover are required in damp moist shade, particularly near water.

B. aconitifolia Z5-8

From West Virginia to Georgia and Alabama in the eastern USA. This has heuchera-like leaves, with dense corymbs of white flowers on stems up to 60cm (24in) high from late spring to midsummer. It is easy to grow in humus-rich soil, preferably acid, and partial shade. Propagate by division in spring or seed in autumn.

B. jamesii (*B. heucheriformis*) Z5

From the north-west USA. A crevice plant for sparse conditions, requiring cool shade and acid soil. Leathery, toothed foliage and crimson flowers in the spring. Often a poor flowerer, it grows to 15cm (6in).

B. rotundifolia Z7

From southern California, as the name suggests this plant has round leaves. Strong growing to 60-90cm (24-36in), it provides good groundcover though it prefers peaty soil. The racemes of white flowers all face one way and they are much in demand by flower arrangers.

JLS86269LACA Sharman

This was originally collected near a mountain stream in southern California. It has tall spikes of many tiny white flowers, with large, round, green calyces. The basal leaves are round and large. It grows up to 1m (40in) high and prefers moist shady conditions and peaty soil.

Chrysosplenium

THE NAME OF THE GENUS, commonly known as golden saxifrage, comes from the Greek for gold and spleen. The plants are natives of acid wet soils and are fine plants for groundcover in moist shade.

C. alternifolium (golden saxifrage) Z4

Spreading by leafless runners and forming carpets of scallop-edged, kidney-shaped leaves. The clusters of tiny golden-green flowers are backed by leafy bracts and are about 10cm (4in) high.

C. davidianum

This flat, spreading plant likes cool shade that does not dry out. The small clusters of bright yellow flowers rise to about 5cm (2in) in summer.

Darmera

THE NAME COMMEMORATES Karl Darmer, the nineteenth-century horticulturist who lived in Berlin. It is a native of north-west California and south-west Oregon.

***D. peltata* AGM** (*Peltiphyllum peltatum*) (umbrella plant, indian rhubarb) Z5
This hardy species is found wild on the banks of mountain streams in its native California and grows best in moist conditions. It will tolerate either sun or shade and makes an ideal marginal water feature. It can also be used in a bog garden or as a bank stabiliser. However, it needs careful placing to obtain the best results from its early flowers, which rise dramatically on unbelievably tall stems, and from the very attractive leaves later in the season. The growth springs from horizontal, scaly, fleshy rhizomes, which first produce the 1-2m (3.5-7ft) high, pink flower stems surmounted by clusters of small rosy blooms. These are followed by dark green serrated leaves 30-60cm (12-24in) in diameter, which have a good autumn colour. The early flowers can be damaged by late frost and some protection might be necessary.

Propagate by division in spring or seed in the autumn or spring. Nurseries usually set cylinders of the rhizome, 4-5cm (1½-2in) long, horizontally in compost in spring, the top surface of the rhizome left exposed. The seed should be sown at a temperature of 16-21 °C (60-70 °F) and kept moist and dark. Seed should germinate in about fourteen days.

***D. p.* 'Nana'**
The dwarf cultivar, 30cm (12in) high and 25cm (10in) across, has round heads of light pink flowers which are followed by long-stalked rounded leaves. Good for the small garden.

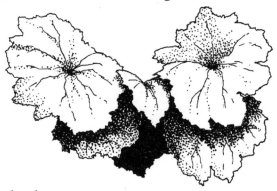

Darmera peltata **leaves**   **Peter Bryan**

Francoa

THIS GENUS IS A NATIVE OF CHILE and was named for Francisco Franco, a sixteenth-century Spanish doctor, who studied botany.

There are several species, though in the British Isles they are not considered to be reliably hardy. They flower in the early summer and sometimes in the autumn. The best position is in full sun and in a well-drained soil; the latter is especially important in the winter.

The plants form rosettes of leaves from which the flowering stems rise and bear wands of dainty rose or white flowers which last for quite a long time. These are strong and do not need staking. The blooms make good cut flowers and as the leaves persist all winter they can be a useful and decorative addition to the border.

Propagation is easy by seed, sown uncovered, preferably as fresh as possible in the autumn at a temperature of 10-13 °C (50-55 °F). Germination is usually good, although it can take up to a month. Plants can also be increased by division in the spring.

The leaf stalks are the main distinguishing feature of the species though some authorities consider them all to be forms of the same very variable species.

F. appendiculata Z9
This plant has graceful wands, made up of small flowers which can be white or pale pink with deep rose markings, on stems up to 60cm (24in) high rising from deeply lobed, dark green petiolate leaves.

F. ramosa (bridal wreath) Z9
This has small, white, spotted flowers in a branched panicle on stems up to 90cm (36in) high. The hairy, lyre-shaped sessile leaves form small clumps which are evergreen. A good cut flower.

F. sonchifolia (bridal wreath) Z8
This also has racemes of pink flowers with darker spotting or blotches on the petals. They rise above lobed evergreen leaves to 75cm (30in) with broadly winged petioles when conditions are good.

It is thought to be the hardiest of this group and has grown successfully in north Lincolnshire, though in a very dry and well-drained spot over a period with mild winters. The plants could be overwintered in a cold greenhouse for greater safety.

Heuchera

THIS GENUS, commonly known as alum root or coral bells, was classified by Linnaeus in 1753 and named after a German professor of medicine J.H. Heucher. The fifty-five native species are found widely spread in North America, mostly in the west and as far south as Mexico.

They are all similar in appearance, having tufts of basal leaves and small, often insignificant flowers. The latter are borne in narrow, loose panicles or racemes on upright stems held above the leaves. Singly they are not very noticeable but in drifts or winding as a continuous thread between other herbaceous plants they can have a delicate impact.

Probably the most important group of hybrids is *H.* × *brizoides* hort. These are complex garden hybrids and are the source of the cultivars and forms and strains that we use in our borders today. Many were originally bred by Lemoine in the nineteenth century but Lemoine only used the name *H.* × *brizoides* for the cultivars resulting from crossing *H. americana* and *H. sanguinea*. However, since then other species have been introduced and the parentage of many of the named varieties has been lost. Academically, this causes headaches for the taxonomist but, happily, gardeners need only rejoice in the proliferation of beautiful and striking plants for their enjoyment. Many new ones are coming on to the market from such breeding programmes as Dan Heims' in the States.

Preferring dappled shade to give of their best, they will survive in less than perfect conditions. A neutral pH coupled with moist humus soil, avoiding clay, is ideal. Some may need a little protection in winter, such as straw or bracken, especially if it is dry. The flowering stems, which make good cut flowers, should be removed when past their best to reveal the decorative foliage, which in many cases is persistent throughout the year.

This group of plants can be invaluable in various garden situations. They can form part of the permanent structure as many are evergreen, and, enjoying partial shade, can produce good groundcover under trees and shrubs. The soft creamy-green flowers of some will act as a foil for a more dramatic feature, while the brilliant pinks and reds of the best cultivars will enhance many border schemes. Striking varieties, such as 'Palace Purple', 'Bressingham Bronze' and 'Pewter Moon', can have an extremely dramatic effect either as 'spot' plants or in bigger groupings to form contrasts – subtle effects with grey foliage or violent statements mixed with orange, red or gold.

Propagation can be by division (best in early autumn but safe in early spring as well) or cuttings taken from some of the old wood. Old crowns tend to rise out of the ground and need mulching or lifting and dividing every third year. Species can, along with some strains, be grown from seed. This is very fine and is best mixed with a base for easier sowing. Leave the seed uncovered and water carefully – by mist spraying if possible. Keep at a temperature of 16-21 °C (60-70 °F) for 30-90 days. Germination is generally not good.

There must be very few gardens that could not use one or more from this genus to great advantage.

Francoa sonchifolia leaves, see page 31   Peter Bryan

H. americana (*H. lucida*, *H. glauca*), (rock geranium, satin leaf) Z4
In cultivation since 1656, this species is mainly grown for its decorative, 15-20cm (6-8in) high foliage, which is tough, leathery and lobed, dark green in colour and coppery veined when young. As the leaves persist it can be useful for the winter garden and it forms good groundcover. The greenish-white flowers appear in the late spring.
'Chocolate Ruffles' D. Heims, 1995
The mat, deeply cut, very ruffled leaves are chocolate on top and burgundy on the underside. The small flowers grow 75cm (30in) high in purple spikes. A very attractive hybrid, it has won several awards.

'Chocolate Veil' D. Heims
This tough hybrid has almost black, smooth leaves with purple highlights. Up to 25cm (10in) across and 30cm (12in) tall.

Dale's Strain D. Hendricks
A seed propagated strain from America, selected for the showy foliage. The leaves are boldly marked with silver and in the autumn variable amounts of maroon veining appear. The small greenish flowers appear in spring and grow 75cm (30in) high. A very tough plant that does well on difficult rocky banks in dry light shade.

'Eco-Improved' D. Jacobs
All the characteristics of 'Eco-Magnififolia' but smoother, larger leaves show an improved contrast and brighter silver.

'Eco-Magnififolia' D. Jacobs
Said to be *H. americana* subsp. *heteradinia*. Semi-evergreen, with dark grey leaves edged with silver and purple veins. The flowers are of the *H. micrantha* type. It is very tolerant of heat and humidity.

'Palace Passion' D. Heims
This hybrid involves *HH. americana*, *sanguinea* and 'Palace Purple'. More sun-resistant than the last, it was the first to combine the chocolate-purple leaves and silver overlay with rose-pink flowers.

'Persian Carpet' D. Heims
The flat leaves are up to 20cm (8in) wide and have metallic shadings on dark red with purple veins and edge. An excellent winter-tolerant foliage plant with *H. micrantha* type flowers.

'Pewter Veil' D. Heims
This semi-evergreen has pewter-purple, 15cm (8in) wide leaves with silver netting between the veins.

H. a. 'Purpurea'
Similar to the species but the undersides of the leaves are marbled brown.

'Ring of Fire' D. Heims
A seedling of *H.* 'Eco-Magnififolia', it is a silver leaved plant suffused with purple along the veins. In autumn the leaves are rimmed a bright coral colour.

'Ruby Ruffles' D. Heims
A cross between 'Ruffles' and 'Pewter Veil', it is very ruffled with a metallic overlay to the ruby leaves and grows to 75cm (30in)

'Ruby Veil' D. Heims
The leaves, 20cm (8in), have metallic slate-grey veination over velvety, ruby-red foliage.

H. a. 'Velvet Night' D. Heims
Dan Heims's darkest cultivar has 20cm (8in) black slate leaves with metallic-purple overlays and 75cm (30in) high flowers. It contrasts well with gold foliage plants.

H. × brizoides hort. Z3
Collectively also known as *Heuchera* Hybrids, these are hybrids of

H. sanguinea and *H. americana,* and possibly also *H. micrantha.* Raised in France in the late-nineteenth century, they will grow in sun or light shade, are hardy and usually free-flowering. The name was originally used for plants with small flowers on slender stems, such as 'Gracillima'.

'Apple Blossom' A. Bloom, 1935
60cm (24in) high with large light pink flowers.

'Bressingham Blaze' A. Bloom, 1950
Sprays of fiery red, large, open bell flowers, 60cm (24in) tall, with marbled leaves.

Bressingham Hybrids A. Bloom
Many strains available: more floriferous, with have pink or red flowers.

'Carmen' A. Bloom, 1950
Intense carmine-pink, medium-sized flowers 60cm (24in) high in spring. It is recommended.

'Charles Bloom' ('Chablo') A. Bloom, 1993
Recently selected and named for Alan Bloom's father. With soft pink, arching sprays.

'Coral Cloud' A. Bloom, 1935
Many small, bright coral-pink flowers, 75cm (30in) high, are borne on large wide panicles in the summer.

'Damask'
Elegant sprays of rich carmine-pink flowers at 50cm (20in)

'Dennis Davidson'
The leaves have dark bronze leaf veins and pale sage highlights. The salmon coloured bells appear in summer, growing to 45cm (18in). Similar to *H.* 'Huntsman'.

'Edge Hall'
A good pink-flowered hybrid. The rather bunched flowerheads suggest *H. cylindrica* in its parentage.

'Feuerregen'
See 'Pluie de Feu'

'Firebird' A. Bloom, 1950
A very good, erect plant bearing many, intense, deep red flowers 60cm (24in) high.

'Freedom' (× *brizoides*) A. Bloom, 1935
Large rose pink flowers on compact sprays to 50cm (20in). Leaves are light green.

'Gloriana' A. Bloom, 1950
The flowers are a bright, deep pink and 60cm (24in) high. It was eventually dropped in favour of 'Carmen'. (A mistake in naming meant that it had also been known as 'Captivation'; though not quite the same, 'Captivation' was dropped as too much like 'Gloriana'.)

'Gracillima' Wallace, 1902
Slender, pink panicles of small flowers 50cm (20in) high are borne in early summer.

'Huntsman'
Clear, bright salmon pink flowers grow to 50cm (20in) from late spring to midsummer, but it is not very free-flowering.

'Ibis' Bloom, 1950
The sturdy sprays bear deep pink blooms from spring to late summer. Originally described as excellent for the front of the border because of its long flowering period.

'Jubilee' A. Bloom, 1935
Named for the Silver Jubilee of George V. Pink flowers, paler than 'Ibis', grow to 50cm (20in) in early summer.

'Lady Romney' A. Bloom, 1953
The small-flowered, soft pink, open panicles bloom 60cm (24in) high in early summer. Marbled leaves.

'Leuchtkäfer' ('Firefly')
This has large panicles of vermilion-red, fragrant flowers, 60cm (24in) high, which are good for cutting. The leaves are hairy.

'Mary Rose' A. Bloom, 1935
The deep pink flowers are 50cm (20in) high.

'Mayfair'
A cross between *H. × brizoides* and *H. hallii*, it is distinguished by small leaves and pink bells 30cm (12in) high.

'Mother of Pearl'
Green and pink flowers grow to 45cm (18in). The dark green leaves are bold and pretty.

'Oakington Jewel' A. Bloom, 1935
Named after Alan Bloom's nursery at Oakington, near Cambridge, its fairly large flowers are a coral-rose colour and grow to 60cm (24in).

'Orphée'
White flowers.

'Pearl Drops' A. Bloom, 1953
As the name suggests, the small flowers are an opalescent white. They are borne on arching sprays 60cm (24in) high.

'Pewter Moon' P. Oudolf
With pewter-marbled foliage, maroon on the reverse, the ice pink flowers reach 30cm (12in) in early summer.

'Pluie de Feu' ('Feuerregen')
Good, persistent, glowing red panicles are borne 60cm (24in) high in midsummer.

'Pretty Polly' A. Bloom, 1953
This has a dwarf habit, 30cm (12in) tall, and very large, clear rose-pink flowers.

'Prûhoniciana'
Named after the Pruhonice Park near Prague, the compact pink flowers, turning to red, rise 50cm (20in) above the persistent leafy cushion base.

'Rachel' M. Ramsdale

A good plant with interest all year. The purple-flushed, dull green-grey leaves have maroon undersides and the red stems bear many small flowers which look like pale pink foam. It blooms for months from spring through to midsummer. 30cm (12in) high.

'Rakete' ('Rocket')

From early summer onwards bright vermilion flowers rise to 60-70cm (24-28in).

'Red Pimpernel'

A vigorous plant bearing 50-60cm (20-24in) high flowers of a scarlet to coral colour.

'Red Spangles' AGM A. Bloom, 1953

The bright scarlet large flowers bloom in the spring and again in late summer on stems 40-60 cm (16-24in) tall.

'Rhapsody'

According to Alan Bloom in 1967 this had the best pink flowers.

'Rosemary Bloom' ('Heuros') A. Bloom

Named for Adrian Bloom's wife. It has coral pink flowers in early summer and a rich-green foliage. 45-60cm (18-24in) high.

'Schneewittchen' ('Snow White')

The white flowers rise above light green variegated leaves in summer. It needs good soil and light shade.

'Shere Variety'

With brilliant scarlet, dainty flower spikes, 45cm (18in) high.

'Silberregen' ('Silver Rain')

The pure white flowers are 50cm (20in) high.

'Silver Veil'

Similar to 'Palace Purple' but the leaf is largely overlaid with silver.

'Sparkler' A. Bloom, 1953

Open light panicles of carmine and scarlet medium-sized flowers, 60cm (24in) high. The leaves are variegated.

'Splendour' A. Bloom, 1953

Salmon to scarlet flowers 45-60cm (18-24in) high. Said to have a poor constitution.

'Sunset' A. Bloom, 1953

This has large, bright red, late blooming flowers, 50cm (20in) high. Not very vigorous.

'Titania'

Very old. Vigorous panicles of salmon pink flowers grow 50-60cm (20-24in) high. Good in exposed positions.

'Weserlachs'

Strong, salmon pink panicles, 60-70cm (24-28in) high, appear early to midsummer.

'Widar'

A vigorous variety with beautiful scarlet flowers 80cm (32in) high.

H. chlorantha Z6
This is a native of British Colombia, Washington and Oregon. Greenish flowers grow to 90cm (36in).

H. cylindrica Z4
This is a native of Nevada, Wyoming, and Montana, west to California and British Columbia. In its natural state it is found on cliffs and rocks. It prefers a well-drained soil. Cylindrical spikes of cream or green flowers 15-90cm (6-36in) high appear in spring through to late summer, but it is usually planted for the foliage. The wavy-edged leaves form dark green mats.

H. c. 'Alba'
A cultivar with cream-coloured flowers.

'Chiqui'
A *cylindrica* hybrid with *sanguinea*, the pink flowers on 45cm (18in) stems rise over compact, slightly hairy leaves.

H. c. 'Greenfinch'
This is a green-flowered selection. A bold, strong grower, with silver-marbled leaves and stiff upright stems 90cm (36in) high. It blooms from spring to midsummer.

'Green Ivory' A. Bloom, 1968
The green blooms, 75cm (30in) high from spring to midsummer, delight the flower arranger. It will not tolerate drought, however. It is a seedling of 'Greenfinch'.

'Hyperion' A. Bloom, 1973
A *H. cylindrica* hybrid. This is short stemmed with soft rosy-red flowers with a hint of green and marbled leaves. Very free-flowering.

'Moondrops' A. Bloom
A *H. cylindrica* hybrid. The leaves are mid-green and lightly silvered. Flowers are a very pale cream with tips tending to pink. Height about 45cm (18in).

H. c. var. alpina
The yellowish-greeny-cream flowers grow 45cm (18in) high and the foliage is pubescent.

H. glabra (*Tiarella colorans*) Z4
A native of Oregon to Alaska, this stoloniferous species has rounded or heart-shaped, deeply lobed leaves which colour in the autumn. It makes good groundcover. Its flowers are 50cm (20in) tall in early summer.

H. grossulariifolia Z5
This is a native of Oregon, Idaho and Montana, USA. It was named in 1900. It is very free flowering and showy, having pure white bell flowers and a height of 10-50cm (4-20in).

H. hallii Z3
Originally from Pikes Peak, Colorado, this is one of the most delicate heucheras with slender 20cm (8in) spikes of white bells in the spring over clumps of small toothed leaves.

H. hispida
See *H. pilosissima.*

H. macrophylla
60cm (24in) high with bronze foliage. Possibly this species has been sunk as it has not appeared in recent works.

H. maritima
This is not a validated name. It was grown from seed by W.E.Th. Ingwersen Ltd. but did not prove to be of any great interest.

H. maxima Z9
A native of California, it is not be quite so hardy. It grows to 60cm (24in) and has white, pink-tinged flowers.

H. micans
This is not a validated name. A heavy bloomer, a 'miniature' with small leaves 2cm (1in) across, it is a very neat plant. Short red stems bear wine-red panicles of white-tinged flowers 15cm (6in) high.

H. merriamii Z7
A low spreading alpine, from California, with greenish flowers to about 20cm (8in).

H. micrantha Z4
A native of western North America, this species has conspicuously attractive grey-marbled leaves and many white flowers with red to orange anthers on stems up to 90cm (36in) high. Blooming in early summer, the seed usually comes true.

'Purple Sails' D. Heims 1996
A hybrid of *H. micrantha* and *H. americana,* the leaves are very dark purple and upright and have a metallic sheen growing to 10cm (4in) across. When mature they spiral into an helix.

'Ruffles'
Ruffled ridges on the woolly leaves form an attractive mound. The small white flowers grow to 60cm (24in).

H. m. var. *diversifolia*
Found from Vancouver Island in British Columbia to North California, it flowers from spring to early summer. The leaves are interesting: they are nearly round in the winter but lobed in the summer.

***H. m.* var. *d.* 'Bressingham Bronze'** ('Absi') A. Bloom
A new cultivar, it is distinct from 'Palace Purple' and has been
vegetatively raised. It has large bronze-purple crinkled leaves which
are bright purple beneath and arching stems of fine, off-white flowers
60cm (24in) high. It blooms from late spring to late summer.

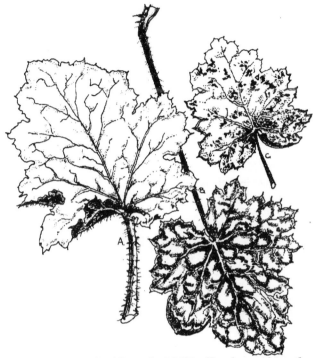

Leaves of *Heuchera cylindrica* 'Greenfinch' (A), *Heuchera micrantha* var.
diversifolia 'Palace Purple' (B), and *Heuchera sanguinea* 'Taff's Joy' (C)

Gwen Grantham

***H. m.* var. *d.* 'Dingle Amber'** M. Handley
Probably from *H. m.* var. *d* 'Palace Purple', as it has similar
characteristics, this was a chance seedling. It has a definite orangey-
brown cast to the leaf and creamy-white flowers.

***H. m.* var. *d.* 'Dingle Mint Chocolate'** M. Handley
Also a chance seedling from 'Palace Purple', this evergreen plant has
large chocolate-brown leaves, edged lime green in the spring but
fading in the summer. It has cream flowers in summer like its parent,
growing to 60cm (24in).

***H. m.* var. *d.* 'Palace Purple' AGM** Introd. B. Halliwell
This colourful variety has very strong blackish-purple leaves,
sometimes with a metallic sheen. The tiny, white flowers are borne

above the foliage. Americans, apparently, are bemused by the popularity of this plant in the UK as in parts of the USA it is considered a weed.

H. m. **var.** *d.* **JLS 86275 CLOR** J. Sharman
The seed was collected in Oregon, USA. The individually tiny white flowers are borne on long brush-like spikes 60cm (24in) high. It is good for a moist, shady bank but will grow in most conditions. The leaves are green with grey or purple markings and can run to form a carpet.

H. parvifolia Z5
This is a native of the Rocky Mountains, from New Mexico to Montana. Cream to white spikes in the summer grow to 38cm (15in).

H. pilosissima (*H. hispida*) Z6
A native of California, it grows in the pine and redwood forests below 300m (1,000ft). It prefers well-drained soil in partial shade. The leaves and stems are hairy, the stems are brown and bear compact racemes of flowers with pinkish-white petals to 55cm (25in).
There is another form of *H. pilosissima* that has white, velvety hairs and grey-pink flowers but it is not considered to be reliably hardy.

H. pringlei
A native of California, this plant likes moist, rich soil. It has a compact, spreading habit and red flowers, growing to 15-20cm (6-8in).

H. procrantzii
Possibly of mid-European origin, it has very small flowers, which create a 'gypsophila' effect in the border.

H. pubescens Z5
A native of central-eastern USA, this species grows to 75cm (30in), with bronze young leaves that colour well in the autumn. The flowers are greenish-white with purple markings.
'Alba'
This is similar to the species but has plain white flowers.
'White Marble' Oliver
A *pubescens* cross, this has huge, white, double-petalled flowers densely packed on 55cm (22in) stems and marbled leaves. It is tolerant of drought.

H. pulchella Z9
From the southern USA and New Mexico, this plant has a very thick rootstock. The margins of the bright green leaves have broad, bristle-tipped teeth. Flowers purple to pink.
SanPico Hybrids Oliver
These plants, crosses between *pulchella* and *hallii*, form low mounds

of small leaves with light pink bell flowers, 25cm (10in) high, in spring on dark coloured stems

JCA 9508 Introd. J. Archibald
Its pink flowers rise to 12cm (5in) and it has neat red-tinted foliage.

H. richardsonii Z5

A native of British Colombia to Colorado and east to Indiana, the flowers are white with purple veins and the foliage is a rich reddish-brown. It grows 60-120cm (24-48in) high. This plant was favoured by Gertrude Jekyll but whether this was the *H. richardsonii* in the National Collection (described as short-stemmed, with heart-shaped leaves with velvety white down, and white flowers) is debateable. Older sources give *H. richardsonii* as a synonym of *H. hispida* and *H. americana*. No doubt the taxonomists will one day clarify this confusion.

H. rubescens

A native of northern California, Nevada and Utah. A good plant for the autumn: the leaves are an old-rose colour, turning copper and dark purple and crimson. The flowers are greeny-buff on short sprays.

'Canyon Delight'
A hybrid of *H. rubescens alpicola* and *H. brizoides,* it has loose sprays of pink flowers on 45cm (18in) stems.

H. sanguinea (coral bells) Z3

This species has been with us since the middle of the nineteenth century and has remained quietly popular. In its native habitats, southern Arizona and north Mexico, it is found among moist, shady rocks. It will thrive in most conditions whether in sun or partial shade in cooler climates. The dark green leaves form low mats, showing off the bright coral-red flowers, 25-50cm (10-20in) high, from spring to autumn. It is a parent of many cultivars, particularly in the hybrid group *H. × brizoides.*

H. s. 'Alba' 1896
This is a white-flowered cultivar of *H. sanguinea.*

H. s. 'Brandon Pink'
Hardy selection with bright coral pink flowers growing to 60cm (24in).

'Frosty' D. Heims
Bright, variegated foliage contrasts well with the deep-red flowers growing to 50cm (20in).

'Grandiflora'
As the name suggests, this vigorous plant has large flowers. The crimson to scarlet flowers are held on 45cm (18in) stems above the leaves.

'Jack Frost'
The rose-coloured flowers complement the very silvered foliage.

H. s. 'Northern Fire'
Hardy selection with deep brick-red flowers over silvered leaves and having a tight habit.
'Robusta'
The flowers are dark red and large.
'Rosea'
Rose coloured flowers about 45cm (18in) high.
'Scintillation' AGM A. Bloom, 1953
From late spring to early summer this bears 60-70cm (24-28in) high flowers of a vivid pink, tipped with carmine. The leaves are marbled with silver. One of Alan Bloom's favourites and a good variety, it has received many RHS awards.
'Silver Veil Improved' D. Heims
Cerise-rose flowers show well against the netted, silver leaves, growing 50cm (20in) high.
'Snow Storm' D. Heims
A *H. sanguinea* hybrid. White leaves edged in green show off the bright cerise flowers growing 45cm (18in) high in the spring. This is a striking plant. It will grow in either sun or partial shade. A warning to country gardeners – it is beloved by rabbits!
'Splendens'
The abundant flowers are a bright carmine red.
'Splish Splash' D. Heims
This is very similar to 'Snow Storm' but brighter.
H. s. 'Taff's Joy'
A very hardy variety, bearing 35cm (14in) high flowers from spring to midsummer. It was found by Stephen Taffler in a garden in Chester, where it appeared spontaneously in a formal planting of *Heuchera sanguinea*. The leaves are speckled and spotted with creamy-white on a grey background, the margins turning pink in winter. It does best in a shaded position in soil enriched with leaf mould.

H. versicolor Z9
A new introduction from New Mexico, USA, this tender plant has greyish foliage and its pink flowers, 15-20cm (6-8in) tall, become rose-red.

H. villosa (alum root) Z6
This comes from the mountains of eastern North America. It prefers well-drained leafy soil in partial shade but will tolerate deep shade and drought. Late to bloom, the loose panicles of pinkish-white flowers are borne 45-60cm (18-24in) high. The huge hirsute leaves are maple-like in shape and often colour well in the autumn.

H. viridis
Pale green flowers and dark green, hairy, scallop-shaped leaves hug the soil and make excellent groundcover.

HYBRID CULTIVARS

'Amethyst Myst' D. Heims, 1996
A veil of silver spreads over the amethyst foliage of this plant and the glossy leaves can make clumps 60 cm (24in) across. A good foliage feature with small white flowers.

'Can Can' D. Heims, 1996
This is the first of the 'ruffles' to take on the metallic silvers forming a tight ruffled mound.

'Canyon Pink' D. Heims, 1996
A very compact plant, the foliage is only 8cm (3in) tall and 30cm (12in) wide. It has good sprays of very deep pink flowers.

'Cappuccino' D. Heims, 1996
The colour of the leaves is creamy-coffee and being sun resistant it mingles well with gold and yellow plants and flowers.

'Cascade Dawn' D. Heims
The lavender shading on the leaves is consistent all season and it makes a good foliage plant.

'Cathedral Windows' D. Heims, 1996
A good foliage plant with full dark leaves showing patches of purple between dark grey veins.

'Mint Julep' D. Heims, 1996
This is a shimmering plant with the brightest silver overlay on the mint-green leaves. A good foliage plant.

'Plum Puddin' Heims, 1996
This has shimmering, plum-purple, shiny foliage and a tight habit, making a good foil for the variegated forms.

'Purple Petticoats' D. Heims, 1996
A good, foliage plant with dark, congested leaves which have purple highlights and burgundy on the underside. Similar to 'Stormy Seas' but with more intensely ruffled leaves.

'Regal Robe' D. Heims, 1996
A compact plant with silver/lavender marbled leaves to 25cm (10in)across. Evergreen and a good specimen plant.

'Silver Shadows' D. Heims, 1996
This is very good for the foliage which is purest dark silver; deep thick and intense with a compact habit and 18cm (7in) leaves.

'Stormy Seas' D. Heims 1995
A striking plant: silver, lavender, pewter and charcoal grey on large heavily ruffled, deeply cut foliage.

'Strawberry Swirl' D. Heims 1995
This looks like a pink bouquet in late spring with up to 60 flower stalks 55cm (22in) high. It is much larger than *sanguinea* and has ruffled fan-like foliage overlaid with silver. Vigorous.

'White Spires' D. Heims, 1996
Clouds of tall, airy, white flowers 75cm (30in) high rise above apple green leaves. It blooms profusely over a long period.

'Whirlwind' Introd. D. Heims, 1996
This has fluted and crested foliage which is bronze-green. It has white flowers and was found in the wild.

'Zabelliana'
The greenish-yellow flowers grow to 60cm (24in) and the leaves are heavily marbled orange-brown when young, later turning green.

× Heucherella

T HESE ARE INTERGENERIC HYBRIDS between various species of the genera *Heuchera* and *Tiarella,* though the majority are *H.* × *brizoides* and *Tiarella cordifolia.* They are complex and sometimes difficult to classify accurately.

Propagation must be by division since these hybrids are sterile. Basal cuttings can be taken in spring or the plants can be divided in the spring or autumn. All are hardy.

× *H. alba* Z3
A soft green, hairy plant with white flowers.
   × *H. a.* 'Bridget Bloom' A. Bloom, 1953
   Tiarella wherryi and *Heuchera* 'Freedom' were used in this cross. A charming little plant with soft green lobed leaves with darker veins clearly marked and elegant sprays of pink-tinged white-petalled flowers 45cm (18in) high. It has a long flowering period from late spring to autumn, preferring light, humus-rich soil in partial shade.
   × *H. a.* 'Pink Frost' C. Oliver
   A selected clone, pink flowers bloom over a long period above lovely frosted foliage. A very popular plant.
   × *H. a.* 'Rosalie'
   A newer selection, it has recurrent pink flowers to 30cm (12in) and evergreen foliage with attractive brown markings.
   × *H. a.* 'White Blush' C. Oliver
   flowers of this selection are white and very pale pink.

× *H. tiarelloides* AGM Lemoine, 1917 Z5
Round, lobed leaves with scalloped edges give rise to brownish scapes of
pink flowers from spring to midsummer. When planted in patches or
drifts they have a light, pink, foamy effect. A dainty and pleasing plant.
  × *H. t.* 'Crimson Clouds'
  A selection with double leaves with crimson dots and good pink
  blooms 40cm (16in) high over a long period.

× *H.* 'Snow White' C. Oliver
This white flowered × *Heucherella* blooms on a compact mound of apple
green foliage.

Lithophragma

T HE NAME COMES FROM THE GREEK for stone and fence,
referring to its native habitat, the Rocky Mountains of North
America. It prefers well-drained peaty soils and shade and has a short
growing season.

L. parviflorum (*Tellima parviflora*) (woodland star)
Its common name describes the white flowers that appear in spring on
stems 40-50cm (16-20in) high though in cultivation it is more usually
20-25cm/8-10in. The green leaves are small but plentiful and parsley-
like in appearance. It prefers good well-drained soil.

Mitella

T HE NAME DERIVES FROM THE LATIN for cap or mitre,
referring to the shape of the fruit; hence the common names,
bishop's cap and mitrewort. It is a native of North America, from
California to British Columbia, and north-east Asia.
    The plants prefer moist shade and make good groundcover, though
they may need a little protection in winter (such as the dry leaves and
small conifer branches found in their native state).

M. breweri Z5
A tufted plant that has small, rounded, bright green, evergreen leaves

with small greenish-yellow flowers on stems 25-30cm (10-12in) high in late spring and summer.

M. diphylla Z3
Found in cool places by streams in woods, it is widespread in eastern North America. It has green, maple-shaped leaves in a basal tuft and slender spires of small, white, star-like flowers 15-30cm (6-12in) high in late spring. It prefers light leafy soil.

Peltoboykinia

THE NAME COMES FROM A GREEK WORD for shield, referring to the shape of the leaves, coupled with *Boykinia*. These two species are natives of the mountainous woodlands of southern Japan.

P. tellimoides (*Boykinia tellimoides*) Z7
From Honshu, Japan. The round leaves tend to face outwards rather than upright; pale green or shiny bronze, they are shallowly lobed or toothed. The petioles, 30cm (1ft) or more tall, attach off-centre in the peltate leaf blades which may be up to 30cm (1ft) across. A good foliage plant near water. In good moist soil and shade it can grow to 1m (40in). The green flowers, however, are insignificant.

P. watanabei
A native of the Japanese islands of Shikoku and Kyushu, this plant is similar to *P. tellimoides* but has longer and wider leaves (long-stalked lobed leaves, acutely dentate) and pale yellow sprays of flowers in the summer. As it is normally found in mountain woods it thrives best in shade.

Rodgersia

THESE PLANTS WERE NAMED for the US Admiral, John Rodgers, who commanded the expedition in which *R. podophylla* was discovered in the 1850s. All of the *Rodgersia* grown in gardens today originated in Japan, China, Korea, Burma or Nepal. They are the largest plants covered by this book and provide good architectural and colourful additions to many garden situations.

In their native habitat they are found growing by streams in shady woodland and can be used in similar ways here, happy in mixed plantings of rhododendrons and ferns or Japanese primulas for instance. They will grow in sun if the soil is permanently moist (a good, humus-rich soil and annual generous mulches help) though they are susceptible to sun-scorch (and wind-scorch) damage. They thrive for Heather Booker, National Collection holder, for example, in a partially shaded 'normal' border, growing with *Hemerocallis*, *Hydrangea aspera* Villosa Group and *Parahebe*. They are not aquatic or marginal plants though and do not like waterlogged soil which means they can be planted around the edges of the artificial ponds so popular at the moment.

The thick rhizomes spread just under the surface of the soil and send up strong long-stemmed leaves to an average height of 1m (40in). These are followed by stately flower spikes, rising above the leaves to form an elegant feature, particularly if grown as a specimen plant. The frothy panicles of flowers, although lacking petals, are colourful, being either cream, pink or red and although the seed pods are small their russet shades in autumn are an added feature. Many of the leaves have a bronze or coppery effect in the spring when they are prone to damage by late frosts. Some colour well in the late summer. The whole plant dies down in winter.

To propagate, either sow seeds in spring or autumn, or divide, preferably in early spring (rather than disturb their roots in winter), by cutting off sections of the rhizomes and potting on (as with *Darmera*) or replanting straight away.

Some species hybridize freely and the seedlings may not be true if in mixed plantings but most will result in good garden subjects. The seed, generally speaking, does not set readily in gardens. Although hardy, they need protection from extremes of heat, drought and wind. Most gardens can benefit from the inclusion of one or more of these fine, robust, striking plants.

R. aesculifolia AGM Z5
From western China. As the name suggests the leaf form is reminiscent of the horse chestnut, being rounded in outline and up to 50cm (20in) across. It grows to 0.7-1.8m (2½-6ft). The stems and leaf veins are brown and pubescent and the white flower panicles arch elegantly downwards in early summer.
'Irish Bronze'
Alan Bloom named this plant, obtained from the Glasnevin Botanic Garden, Dublin in the late 1950s. It has white flowers and bronze foliage. A good clone, though possibly a form of *R. pinnata* or a hybrid.

R. henrici Z6
This was named in 1897 by Adrian Franchet to commemorate Prince

Henri d'Orléans, a grandson of Louis Philippe, who travelled extensively in Yunnan, where he found *R. henrici* in 1895. There is much controversy about this species and many plants sold under this name are a hybrid. The distinguishing feature of the species, that the sepals do not grow longer after pollination, is hardly likely to excite the average gardener! It is less common than *R. aesculifolia*, which it resembles closely, and occurs further south in the wild – it has been found in south-west Tibet and Upper Burma, where Kingdon Ward described it as bright pink and fragrant.

The flower can vary in colour from greenish-white to rosy-pink, the plumes appearing in late spring. The leaves are strongly veined and textured, and sometimes give good autumn colour. It is easy to grow given moist soil in sun or partial shade. There are fine examples in the Royal Botanic Garden at Edinburgh.

R. nepalensis (*R. nepalense*)
This is now starting to be available. It is a distinct species, widely separated geographically from the rest of the genus. With 7-11 pinnate leaflets as in *R. sambucifolia*, with long hairs along the petioles and on the undersides of the leaves and a distinct coppery edge in spring, it has loosely branched panicles of greenish-white flowers.

R. pinnata Z5
Found in the shady moist margins of mixed pine forest in Yunnan and Sichuan, it is a variable species – both in the wild and in gardens. A showy plant it has dark green glossy leaves made up of 6-9 leaflets (it is not pinnate but either pseudopinnate or palmate). The leaves of most forms have a wrinkled surface and are bronze when young, turning green with age. Originally described as the stem having yellow silky hairs at the insertion of the leaves and at its base. The flower panicle is branched and up to 1m (40in) high and usually pinkish but it can vary. Most flowers on the inflorescence open by late spring and the sepals gradually and imperceptibly turn into seed heads. Several cultivars are available.

R. p. 'Alba' Introd. Wilson, 1905
This comes from Sichuan. It has yellowish-white flowers.

R. p. 'Buckland Beauty'
This sometimes has a flat corymb of rose-red flowers, which is most distinctive.

R. p. 'Elegans'
A choice plant with majestic ribbed foliage and graceful scented flowers, creamy-white to pink. It grows to 90cm (36in).

R. p. 'Maurice Mason'
Christopher Lloyd named this clone for M. Mason from whose garden he had obtained it. It is tall and vigorous (unlike 'Superba'), growing to 1.2m (4ft). It flowers freely, over a long period, producing

pink flowers from late spring to autumn.

R. p. 'Rosea'
A specimen is currently in the National Collection held by Heather Booker. The colour of the inflorescence is similar to 'Superba'.

R. p. 'Rubra'
This has deep red flowers. This is mentioned by Jellito and Schacht but has so far remained elusive to other collectors and sources.

R. p. 'Superba' AGM
This is a taller-growing cultivar. It has shiny dark green leaves, thickly textured with veins 'sunk' below the surface giving a quilted effect. The outer parts of the sepals are paler but the overall effect is of bright pink flowers, dark red stems and dark red seed capsules. An excellent and dramatic garden plant, in time forming large clumps. It is an indirect parent of 'Kupfermond' bequeathing its very coppery foliage.

Yet another debate simmers about this *Rodgersia* as some authorities consider it to be *R. henrici*. 'Superba' seems to differ from the species *R. pinnata* in that most leaves are palmate except that the central leaflet has a 3-4mm stalk, though it occasionally produces pseudopinnate leaves. However, there are other experts equally convinced that 'Superba' is simply another variant on the very variable *R. pinnata* theme. Alternatively, it might be a hybrid between the two species.

CLD0432
Collected on the Kew, Edinburgh and RHS expedition to the Yunnan province of China in 1990. The fruiting heads are reddish in colour.

R. podophylla AGM (*R. japonica*) Z5
A distinct species from Japan and Korea. Glossy leaves over 50cm (20in) across are made up of 5 leaflets, usually with tri-sectional apices, occasionally more. This characteristic distinguishes it from other *Rodgersia*. The foliage is bronze when young, turns deep green and then bronze again in the autumn. The yellowish-white nodding panicles reach about 2m (7ft) in late spring and early summer. Some consider this the best species for flowers. Good autumn colour.

Slieve Donard form
This is similar to the species but runs about more.

'Pagode' E. Pagels, 1972
The white flowers turn green and have large panicles. The leaves have wide marginal serrations giving a 'frilly' appearance to the leaflets.

'Parasol'
Probably a hybrid with *R. aesculifolia*.

'Rotlaub' ('Red Leaves') E. Pagels, 1976
It has creamy-white flowers, and green leaves suffused with mahogany.

'Smaragd' ('Emerald') E. Pagels
This has white flowers and green leaves.

R. purdomii Z6
It is claimed that the name has never been officially published though it is in common useage. It is thought to have come from China by William Purdom who collected for Kew in the 1920s. It is about 90cm (36in) high and has attractive palmate coppery foliage – in some cultivars, such as 'Werner Mueller', it is very pronounced. It has pure white flowers from late spring to midsummer.

R. sambucifolia Z6
This has a true pinnate leaf, with 7-9 leaflets or more, and flat-topped panicles of white or pink flowers. It is usually smaller than the other species of the genus and has a more delicate appearance – larger plants with this name may be hybrids with R. pinnata.

R. sp. CLD 1329
Collected on the Kew, Edinburgh and RHS expedition to China, 1990, it was found growing with rhododendrons in the Yunnan. It has upright panicles of creamy-white flowers in early summer. The leaves are pinnate and bright green with little trace of red – new leaves are sometimes damaged by frost. Height up to 75cm (30in). Moist soil in the sun.

R. sp. CLD 1432
Also collected on the Kew, Edinburgh and RHS expedition to the Yunnan in 1990, it has been suggested that this is R. henrici. It has palmate leaves and grows to 90cm (36in).

RECENT GERMAN INTRODUCTIONS
According to Heather Booker, National Collection Holder of rodgersias, there are some beautiful cultivars and hybrids coming from Germany, mostly derived from R. pinnata.

'Blickfang' ('Eyecatcher') 1985
The new leaves in spring are reddish and grow to 1m (3ft), with a reddish tinge over the green later in the year. The rose red flowers on salmon red stems rise to 1.3m (4¼ft). The seed pods are also red and persist in winter.

'Elfenbeinturm' ('Ivory Tower') 1988
1.8m (6ft) tall with 1m (40in) foliage surmounted by a branched flowerhead. The large green leaves with green stems support pink buds fading to ivory with a faint vanilla scent. It is a dramatic plant for single exhibition and very impressive.

'Ideal' 1987
A delicately formed plant, 1.1m (44in) high, with red-edged, dark green leaves. New growth is reddish and red flowers give way to red seed pods.

'Kupfermond' ('Coppermoon') 1987

The creamy-white flowers borne on red stems 1.6m (5ft) high above the light-green deeply-toothed leaves give a striking contrasting effect. (It is good for brightening dark shady spots.) The seed pods are copper red. Even with late frosts this cultivar is reliable and floriferous in late spring.

'Maigrün' ('Maygreen') 1991

Greenish-white flowers give a lacy filigree effect. The leaves and seed heads are lime green and the whole plant has a delicate spring-like appearance.

'Rosenlicht' ('Rose Light') 1991

Grows to 1m (40in) with shiny foliage. It is late blooming; the rose-pink buds turn to white flowers with pink centres, so extending the season.

'Rosenzipfel' ('Rose Tip') 1992

1.2m (4ft) pink inflorescences turning in at the tips give a distinctive appearance. It has greenish-red foliage and red stems.

'Roter Zwerg' ('Red Dwarf') 1988

Low growing, 80cm (32in), this has dark rose-red buds and flowers that turn paler with age on red stems. The seed pods are also red and the foliage is green with a red shimmer.

'Rothaut'

A hybrid of *sambucifolia* and *pinnata* with scarlet stems, green leaves and white flowers.

Saxifraga

A large and varied genus, it is native to the arctic and mountainous regions of Europe, Asia and North America. Growing in crevices (the name comes from the Latin *saxum*, rock, and *fragere*, to break) the plants were supposed to be capable of breaking rocks – hence their alleged medicinal property for gall stones.

While most of the saxifrages are more suitable for the rock or alpine garden the following can provide useful and attractive additions to some herbaceous situations. They can be invaluable for tucking into inhospitable corners where other plants would perish. A tidy edge of London pride around a rose bed or along the path side of a mixed border can look good. Saxifrages can also be used for groundcover, taking advantage of their natural manner of growth to cover a shady bank. Being generally evergreen, they can add structure and help define the garden in the winter.

Generally, all the saxifrages can be propagated vegetatively, taking rooted offsets in winte; *Saxifraga fortunei*, however, is best divided in the spring. Seed should be sown in the autumn at a temperature of 60-70 °F or 16-21 °C and may take up to 90 days to germinate. E.A. Bowles, who held *S. fortunei* in high regard, emphasised that as it flowers so late it seldom has time to set seed. He suggested that a plant be potted up and given some protection until the seed is ripe, for it is very slow to increase by division.

The genus is fairly free from pests and diseases, although slugs and snails can attack the foliage. There have been attacks of vine weevil recorded too.

There are few gardens that could not find a welcome place for these familiar little plants.

S. cuscutiformis (*S. stolonifera* var. *minor*) Z5

This makes good groundcover with loose leaf rosettes and thread-like red stolons. The leaves are a browny-green and well marked, shaggy with glossy red undersides. The large white flowers grow 20cm (8in) tall in late summer. Tolerant of dry shade, this will even grow under yew trees.

S. fortunei AGM (*S. cortusifolia* var. *fortunei*) Z7

This native of Japan, Korea, E. Siberia and N. China, grows on wet shady rocks and flowers from early summer to autumn. It was first introduced in 1863.

The red stems can reach a height of 45cm (18in) and have small white flowers rising above round veined waxy leaves which are green above and pinkish-brown underneath. This species flowers later than the others; it succumbs to the first frost and all but disappears but it is very hardy and will come forth again in the spring. It prefers a moist situation, shaded from strong sunshine.

'Obtusocuneata'

Similar to *S. fortunei* but with smaller leaves that are green with purple undersides. The small white flowers grow 10cm (4in) high in late autumn. It prefers an acid soil and shade.

S. f. 'Wada' ('Wada's Variety') K. Wada

This is not a 'red' plant but has leaves that are shiny bronze on top and dark pink beneath. It is often confused with 'Rubrifolia'. Both are very attractive additions to the garden.

Between the First and Second World Wars there was a considerable trade in plants from Japan, particularly from Koichiro Wada (1911-81) who raised this lovely form (he was awarded an Honorary Fellowship by the RHS in 1965).

S. f. 'Rubrifolia'

Similar to the previous plant but the flowers are snow-white and form a good contrast to the glossy red stems and red-brown leaves. The whole plant has a reddish hue.

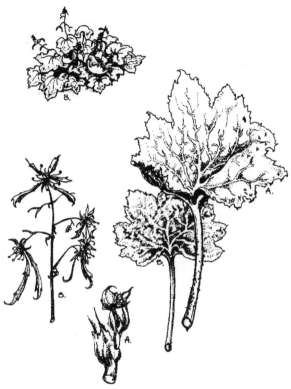

Saxifraga fortunei (A) and *S. f.* 'Wada' (B) see overleaf   **Gwen Grantham**

S. × *geum* Z3
This hybrid of *hirsuta* and *umbrosa* has long been considered a species with intermediate characteristics between the parents.
'Dentata'
This is similar to London pride in many respects but has a very good, succulent looking dentate-shaped leaf. It is happy in sun or shade, damp or dry conditions and makes good groundcover or front of the border plant.

S. *hirsuta* (rough-leaved rockfoil)
This is a native of south-west Ireland, the Pyrenees and northern Spain. Easily grown given its natural habitat of moist shady places, it is not tolerant of drought. It prefers good humus-rich soil. It forms hairy-

leaved mats of loose persistent rosettes from which rise pubescent stems of white flowers up to 30cm (12in) high.

***S. stolonifera* AGM** (mother of thousands, strawberry geranium) Z6
This native of western China and Japan is found on shady cliffs and mossy rocks. Rosettes of fleshy leaves. White star-shaped flowers (with irregularly shaped petals giving a 'shooting star' effect) grow to 40cm (16in) in late spring-early summer. It spreads by long red stolons and is easily grown in moist shade or as a house plant.

'Tricolor' AGM
Very similar to *S. stolonifera* but the leaf has green, pink and white markings and is coarse and hairy. 15cm (6in) tall, sparse, white flowers in late summer.

S. umbrosa (porcelain flower, Jehovah's flower) Z6
This native of the western and central Pyrenees (and Yorkshire) was described by W. Keble Martin as having oval leaves with obtuse teeth, with the terminal tooth being shorter and broader, the petiole is shorter than the blade and very ciliate.

It forms close carpets of flat rosettes of leathery leaves and bears white, red-spotted flowers in mid-to-late spring. It is easily cultivated.

Care is required when identifying this plant, however, as almost all thought to be *S. umbrosa* are actually *S.* × *urbium*.

S. *u*. var. *primuloides*

'Clarence Elliott' AGM ('Elliott's Variety')
This is compact, very free-flowering with red stalks and pink flowers which rise to about 20cm (8in). It flowers in mid-spring.

Jack Elliott (nurseryman, garden journalist and founder member of the Alpine Garden Society) found this plant with its unusually deep pink flowers and dwarf habit in the Alps before the First World War. He exhibited it at a RHS show under the name 'Elliott's Variety' to find that Walter Ingwersen was showing a similar plant called 'Ingwersen's Variety' (see below). Though markedly alike they have continued to sell under their respective names.

'Walter Ingwersen' ('Ingwersen's Variety')
Small with bronze leaves and red-stemmed, dark pink flowers. Good among ferns.

***S.* × *urbium* AGM** (*S. spathularis* × *S. umbrosa*) G. London Z6
Commonly known as London pride, this well-known plant soon forms a tidy dark-green carpet sending up flower stems 30cm (12in) high in mid-to-late spring. The starry blooms, although tiny, are very attractive and close inspection reveals their prettily coloured markings.

According to Dr Prior's *Popular Names of British Plants*, a Mr Howard asserted in the *Gardener's Chronicle* that this plant got its name from

George London, from the firm of London and Wise (the celebrated royal gardeners of the early-eighteenth century) who introduced it into cultivation.

Easily grown and widely planted, this popular little plant is probably the best known of all the saxifrages.

S. × u. 'Aureopunctata'
This has yellow blotches on the leaves and is not quite so vigorous. Starry pink flowers in spring, 30cm (12in) high.

S. × u. 'Colvillei'
Neat serrated leaves with white flowers.

'Letchworth Gem'
This closely resembles the well-known London pride but the leaves are rounder and the flower spikes are shorter and slightly darker in colour. Spring-flowering, it builds up quickly amd makes a useful addition to the front of the border or as groundcover.

'Miss Chambers'
Very pretty, with dainty rosy-pink flowers which are taller than London pride and with a longer flowering period. Glossy leaves.
Valerie Finnis received this plant from a Miss Chambers and it then went to Pamela Schwerdt and Sibylle Kreutzberger. It has proved a popular addition to gardens ever since and looks well in the Rose Garden at Sissinghurst.

'Variegata'
Has white variegated leaves with pink-tinged edges.

Tanakaea

THE GENUS WAS NAMED for the botanist, Yoshio Tanaka (1838-1916), and is native to the Japanese islands of Shikoku and Kyushu where it is found on wet, rocky sites in shade.

T. radicans Z8
This makes a small low mound and prefers an acid soil. The deep green, serrated leaves are greyish on the undersides and evergreen. The flowers are borne on short, hairy stems and form small creamy-white plumes 15cm (6in) high in early summer. Though rare it is a good easy plant for well-drained acid soils in the rock or woodland garden.

Tellima, Tiarella
and Tolmiea

INTRODUCTION
Judy Harry

These genera tend to be regarded as unassuming and useful rather than exciting but they have much more to offer the gardener than this description would suggest. They are all pretty and have among their number some very fine foliage plants.

All bear particularly descriptive common names. *Tellima* is known as fringe cups, emphasising the charm of the individual flowers, each one of which has a fringed rim. Foam flower is the popular name for *Tiarella cordifolia*, whose airy white flowers seem to foam over the ground once a good-sized patch of the plant has become established. With *Tolmiea*, the common name, pick-a-back plant, perfectly describes the way in which small plantlets form on mature leaves as if having a pick-a-back ride.

They are relatively late introductions to British gardens: *Tiarella* reached Europe in the mid-eighteenth century and *Tellima* and *Tolmiea* arrived in the nineteenth. With the exception of *Tiarella polyphylla*, they are natives of North America, where their habitat is moist woodland, either deciduous or coniferous. This obviously makes them useful plants for semi-shaded positions in the garden, where they will also tolerate quite a range of other conditions.

Their attraction lies primarily in the contrast that exists between the substantial leaves and the very dainty inflorescences. Each complements the effect of the other and are most effective when grown in drifts or large groups. The prettily-shaped leaves of all three genera, and the interesting colouring of some, make them ideal foils and contrast for more flamboyant border plants. They flower quite early in the summer to make a useful contribution before the main flush of summer colour.

As *Tellima* and *Tolmiea* are evergreen, they help to give interest to the winter garden and *Tellima* can be used to great effect in containers planted for winter interest.

TELLIMA

Tellima is an anagram of the closely related *Mitella*. Several species once classified as *Tellima* have been transferred to *Lithophragma*.

These hardy perennials form clumps of prettily-shaped, hairy leaves with long spikes of small flowers in spring and early summer. They are happy in either sun or shade and are useful under shrubs. They remain fairly small, 45-60cm (18-24in) high, when in bloom and persist in the winter.

They can be propagated either by seed, division, or by potting the tiny plantlets when they appear. Seed should be planted in the autumn at a temperature of 13-18 °C (55-65 °F) and can take between thirty and ninety days to germinate.

T. breviflora Z6
It can be found from British Columbia to northern California, where it grows by streams and flowers in the spring. Similar to *Tellima grandiflora*, some consider it to be the same species.

T. grandiflora Z4
Long spikes of green and pink flowers rise 60-75cm (24-30in) above the green hairy leaves which persist in both summer and winter.

Tellima grandiflora embraces several groups including Alba, Odorata and Rubra.

T. g. **Alba Group**
These have white flowers.

T. g. **Odorata Group**
This group has pale yellowish-green scented flowers.

'Perky' JLS86282SCCA Sharman
This is a wild-collected form with red petals. The flower spikes and leaves are smaller than usual and so it has a very dainty appearance.

T. g. **'Purpurea'**
This variety has pink flowers and attractive coppery-purple leaves in the autumn and winter. Possibly not distinct from the Rubra Group.

T. g. **'Purpurteppich'**
This differs in that the leaves become veined and stained maroon in summer. The flowers have dark stems and pink-stained rims to the large green bells, 60cm (24in) high, blooming in mid-to-late spring.

T. g. **Rubra Group**
Long spikes of green and pink flowers rise 60-75cm (24-30in) above leaves that turn a strong reddish-purple in the winter. It is sometimes scented.

T. parviflora
See *Lithophragma parviflora*.

T. **'Forest Frost'** D. Heims, 1996
Found in a native population, this is a silver-splashed leaved form which looks particularly good in the autumn when the background colour turns burgundy. The chartreuse flowers fade to pink. It tolerates both shade and drought.

TIARELLA

The name derives from the description of the fruit which resemble little tiaras. Commonly known as false mitrewort or sugar scoop, the genus can be found in eastern and north-west North America.

T. californica
Found in California, it is almost unknown in horticulture. It is similar to *Tiarella unifoliata* (maybe indistinct from) being about 30cm (12in) high with white flowers.

T. collina
See *T. wherryi* Collina Group.

T. cordifolia AGM (foam flower) Z3
It can be found in the rich, moist soils of mountainous woodlands from Nova Scotia to Alabama and west to Minnesota.

Clump-forming, though the more vigorous selections make large spreading mats from stolons. The simple, rarely branched, 15-20cm (6-8in) high racemes bear profuse white flowers in spring. The pale green leaves sometimes have dark markings and the veins turn bronze-red in winter. As the foliage is persistent it can make a valuable contribution to the garden all through the year. Preferring cool shade, it does not like very dry conditions and will die back if the ground dries out.

T. c. 'George Shenk Pink'
This is a compact selection with unmarked leaves. The rich pink flowers, darker in colour than normal, bloom later.

'Glossy' D. Jacobs
This American hybrid has large, bright green, evergreen leaves and white flowers. Good plant for the future.

T. c. 'Lilacina'
Pale lilac flowers.

T. c. 'Major'
Salmon-rose to wine-red flowers.

T. c. 'Marmorata'
The leaves are bronze-gold turning dark-green mottled purple, with reddish flowers.

T. c. 'Purpurea'
Foliage and flowers are purple-tinged, the latter have maroon petioles.

T. c. 'Slick Rock' J. Plyler
A new selection, found near Slick Rock Creek, North Carolina. An evergreen plant with short small leaves and a running habit, it spreads faster than any other maple-leaved *Tiarella*. White flowers grow to 20cm (8in).

T. c. subsp. *collina*
See *T. wherryi* Collina Group.

Tiarella cordifolia (to rear) and *Tolmiea menziesii*   **Sally Grant**

T. laciniata Z4
A rare species, occurring naturally from Alaska to Oregon in North America. The rhizomes are slender and creeping and the leaves completely divided. The flowers are white in loose panicles.

T. polyphylla Z7
A native of Sikkim, Bhutan, western China, Taiwan and Japan, it prefers moist shady banks in light woodland and spreads by underground stolons. The flower stems rise to 10-40cm (4-16in) and bear white, pink or green blooms in narrow racemes from spring to late summer.

Pink form Introd. M. Rix
This has pink flowers.

60

Pink form 'Axminster Variegated' CRD Plants
Comes true from seed: clump-forming, growing to 30cm (12in) with
pink flowers but has white-splashed leaves in spring.
White form A. Schilling
Collected in the the Himalaya. White flowers, which are pink in bud,
contrast with the new pale green seed capsules. Good plant.
***T. p.* 'Moorgrün'**
Rampageous – it soon makes a carpet of soft green in part or full
shade. White flower spikes in the spring grow to 15cm (6in).

T. trifoliata Z5
A native of Oregon, north to Alaska, and east to Montana and parts of
Idaho. It favours damp woodland, particularly near streams. Clump
forming with ivy-shaped leaves, it blooms from spring to summer. The
flowers display a starry effect and rise to 25-50cm (10-20in).
'Incarnadine'
This is an unusual pink form.
'Filigree Lace' C. Oliver
A cross of *T. trifoliata* and 'Tiger Stripe', this is a non-running form
with white flowers and lacily-cut leaves similar to *T. trifoliata* var.
laciniata. The leaves are dark red in late autumn and the flowers are
light pink and 30cm (12in) tall.
'Martha Oliver' M. & C. Oliver
A good plant, a trifoliate hybrid, with white flowers 35-45cm (14-
18in) high in late spring. The divided green leaves are glossy with
maroon markings which vary seasonally in intensity, usually turning a
good red in the autumn. It is vigorous and soon makes a large open
clump.

T. unifoliata Z3
Found from Alaska to California, it is not stoloniferous and the hairy
lobed leaves are brownish when young turning dull green later. The
white, loose-flowered panicles are 20-30cm (8-12in) high. Not vigorous.

T. wherryi AGM Z3
The neat small clumps are topped by white flowers to 15cm (6in). The
maple shaped leaves have a velvet like texture.
'Bronze Beauty' C. Brickell
This is a typical *wherryi* but it does display some variations. From a
slow-growing clump forming mounds of triangular hairy basal leaves,
stained dark red, racemes of pink or white fragrant flowers arise in the
spring. These give way in autumn to russet or brown coloured foliage.
Collina Group (*T. collina*, *T. cordifolia* subsp. *collina*)
It integrates with the typical *T. wherryi* and cannot be treated as a

separate botanical entity. A native of Tennessee, North Carolina and Alabama, it is found in shady ravines and rocky woods. Each plant forms small patches about 20cm (8in) round. The flowers which appear in midsummer are 15-35cm (6-14in) high and tinted purple. Preferring cool shelter it is an attractive addition to the border.

T. w. 'Elizabeth Oliver' M. & C. Oliver
This intensely coloured selection from the USA, with pink flowers and dark green leaves, grows 30-40cm (12-16in) high in late spring.

T. w. 'Fig-leaf'
This uncommon *wherryi* form from the USA has deeply-lobed, fig-like leaves with a conspicuous, central, maroon patch. The flowers are pink and grow 30-40cm (12-16in) high.

T. w. 'Oakleaf'
This selection is similar to the fig-leaved hybrid. The foliage is burgundy in winter. Very pale pink flowers fade to white in early spring.

T. w. 'Pink Foam' B. Chatto
This *wherryi* was found to differ slightly from the typical form: the leaves are slightly longer and darker.

T. w. 'Tiger Stripe' M. & C. Oliver
A very vigorous selection from the USA from crosses involving three species of the eastern foam flower. The glossy foliage is unmarked in the spring but maroon markings develop later in the summer, turning dark red in late autumn. The flowers are light pink and grow 36-45cm (14-18in) high. It in non-running and very showy.

Hybrid Cultivars

'Dark Eyes' D. Heims
A compact plant with spreading foliage. Each dark maple-shaped leaf has a heavy blotch of black, giving bronze tones in winter.

'Dark Star' D. Heims
The star-shaped leaves have very dark centres. This is a strong flowerer to 35cm (14in) and makes attractive mounds.

'Freckles' D. Heims
This has a different leaf pattern to the usual *Tiarella*, being partially cut and speckled with purplish brushstrokes. The flowers are tall.

'Inkblot' D. Heims
This has the deepest black patches on the leaves and white flowers 30cm (12in) high. Its habit is tight and non-running.

'Pink Bouquet' D. Heims
Excellent for colour, form and fragrance, this plant has very attractive pink 'foamy' flowers held above green foliage.

'Pin Wheel' D. Heims
A new unique form, showing the tailored *Tiarella* shape with lightly

painted leaves cut to the centre and overlapping like a pinwheel. It has a good flowering habit.

'Skeleton Key' D. Heims
This has cut leaves unlike any other form and makes a good foliage plant for containers. The flowers grow to 25cm (10in).

TOLMIEA

This genus was named for Dr William Frazer Tolmie (1812-86), a surgeon with the Hudson Bay Company. It is found growing naturally in the cool shade of the coniferous forests of western North America, from Alaska to California.

It forms large clumps of pale green hairy leaves from which rise stems of brown flowers to a height of 30-80cm (12-32in) in mid-to-late spring and intermittently during the summer. Soon colonising large areas it can make convenient groundcover, and, as it is persistent, contributes to the winter garden. Though not fussy about soil type, it does not like to dry out. Although individually insignificant, the flowers can be appreciated when viewed in large patches.

The cultivation requirements are few. Plant or divide in either autumn or spring, preferably in a well-drained, humus-rich soil in sun or partial shade. It needs protection from excessive sun because of possible leaf scorch.

Propagation can be effected by pegging the leaves down into soil, where they will root. Small plantlets can be found 'cradled' in some leaves and these will usually root well if detached and put in a good potting medium.

Another good feature of this plant is its ability to survive and thrive indoors as a pot plant. Generally free from pests and diseases.

T. menziesii **AGM** Z7
From creeping rhizomes, maple-like, mid-green leaves rise, followed by the flower spires, which are sometimes greenish-white, flushed red or brown.

'Taff's Gold' **AGM** ('Goldsplash', 'Maculata', 'Variegata')
Variable attractive cream- or gold-mottled markings can lighten a dark corner. It is also more compact in habit than the species.

JLS 86284CLOR J. Sharman
In early summer, spikes of purple-brown flowers rise above soft, hairy green leaves to a height of 45cm (10in). It will thrive in any soil that does not dry out in summer. The leaves can be frost sensitive in early spring and although it is less persistent in winter than the species it is similar in habit, and taller than 'Taff's Gold'.

Pests and Diseases

GENERALLY SPEAKING, the Saxifragaceae are relatively free from infestation.

Leafy Gall (*Rhodococcus fascians* syn. *Corynebacterium fascians*)
This bacterium is very widespread and causes galls on a wide range of plants. The pathogen lives in the soil and the exact means of infection is uncertain (in some cases it could be transmitted by seed). It causes stems with masses of short or thickened shoots, especially near ground level. Destroy the affected plants and do not plant susceptible species in contaminated land for as long as possible. Disinfect hands, tools and pots and use sterilised compost.

Vine Weevil (*Otiorhynchus sulcatus*)
This pest can be a problem, especially for plants grown in containers. The adult weevil is black, measures 10-12mm long and hides in the top layers of the soil. They start to feed in May and lay eggs about four weeks later through to late September. The eggs are laid around the host plant root system. When they hatch they feed on the roots. They overwinter in the host plant often killing it and pupate in the spring, the adults emerging to feed on the foliage. Try to avoid its introduction by carefully inspecting the roots of newly-obtained plants before planting. If in doubt remove all the soil before planting. *Boykinia*, *Darmera* and *Francoa* appear to be less affected but they are still susceptible.

There are encouraging reports of good control by nematodes (*Steinernema carpocapsae* for the control of the larvae) which are environmentally friendly. Proprietary products include Ciba Bunting's Exhibit SC-WDG, Zeneca's Nature's Friends, Bio-safe and Suscon Green.

Rust (*Puccinia pazschkei*)
Occasionally this manifests itself. It is probably widespread in gardens but requires a trigger, such as certain weather conditions, to become active. Dark red-brown pustules burst through the upper leaf surfaces. Damage is rarely severe but it is best to destroy badly affected plants.

Slugs and snails
They may attack some members of the Saxifragaceae where the leaves come into contact with the soil.

Nurseries and Gardens

THE *RHS PLANT FINDER* (edited by Tony Lord and published annually by Moorland Publishing, Ashbourne, Derbyshire) tells where plants can be obtained. The following nursery addresses (with an indication of the range of plants on offer) are included since they are less easily obtained in the UK. MO indicates that mail order is available.

Belgium
Dennis Dujardin, Landschapsarchitect, Jan Breydellaan 47, B - 8500 Kortrijk. Tel: 056.21.92.50. Astilbes, francoas, heucheras and tellimas.

Germany
Georg Arends, Staudenkulturen, Monschaustraße 76, D-5600 Wuppertal 21. Tel: 202.464610. Very good selection of astilbes listed. MO
Hans Götz, Staudengärtnerei, D-7622 Schiltach. Tel: 7836.93980. Good selection of astilbes, bergenias and heucheras listed. MO
Heinrich Hagemann, Staudenkulturen, Walsroder Straße324, D-3012 Langenhagen-Krähenwinkel. Tel: 511.737644. Good selection of astilbes listed. MO
Heinz Klose, Staudengärtnerei, Rosenstraße 10, D-3503 Lohfelden. Tel: 561.515555.Very good selection of astilbes, bergenias and heucheras listed. MO
Uwe Knöpnadel, Friesland Staudengarten, Husumer Weg 16, D-2942 Jever 3 (Rahrdum). Tel: 4461.3763. Outstanding selection of astilbes, bergenias, heucheras and rodgersias listed. MO
Peter & Bärbel zur Linden, Osnabrücker Staudenkulturen, Linner Kirchweg 2, D-4516 Bissendorf 1 (Linne). Tel: 5402.5618. Good selection of astilbes and recent introductions of rodgersias listed. MO
Hans & Helga Simon, Sortiments und Versuchsgärtnerei, Staudenweg 2, D-8772 Marktheidenfeld. Tel: 9391.3516. MO – 10 astilbes, 29 bergenias, 10 heucheras, 11 rodgersias, 5 t listed.

Netherlands
Eric Holterman & Erwin Velthuis, De Border, Twickelerlaan 13, 7495 VG Ambt-Delden. Tel: 5407.64123/63897. Fax: 5407.64950. Very good selection of astilbes, bergenias and heucheras listed.
D.J. Ploeger, Th. Ploeger en Zu BV, Blauwkapelseweg 73, 3731 EB De Bilt. Tel: 30.202602. Fax: 30.204494. Very good selection of astilbes, bergenias, heucheras and rodgersias listed.
N.A.Rijnbeek, Rijnbeek en Zoon, Reijerskoop 303, 2771 BL Boskoop. Tel: 1727.12549. Fax: 1727.18131. Very good selection of astilbes, bergenias and heucheras listed.

USA

Busse Gardens, 13579 - 10th Street NW, Cokato MN 55321. Tel: 612.286.2654. Outstanding selection of astilbes and bergenias listed.
Carroll Gardens, 444 East Main Street, P.O. Box 310, Westminster MD 21157. Tel: 301.848.5422. Very good selection of astilbes listed.
Tony & Michelle Avent, Plant Delight Nursery, 9241 Sauls Road, Raleigh, NC 27603. Tel: 919.772.4794. New cultivars heucheras and tiarellas.
Dan Heims, Terra Nova Nurseries, B&B Laboratories, 1600 D. Dunbar road, Mt Vernon, WA 98273. New cultivars of heuchera, heucherella and tiarella.
Martha and Charles Oliver, The Primrose Path, R.D.2 Box 110, Scottdale, PA 156 83. New cultivars of tiarella and heuchera.

NATIONAL PLANT COLLECTIONS

Supplementary information has been taken from *The National Plant Collections Directory 1995*, published by the NCCPG (The Pines, Wisley Garden, Woking, Surrey, England GU23 6QB. Tel:01483.211465) at £2.95.

Astilbe
Henry Noblett, Ullswater Road, Windermere, Cumbria LA23 1NP.
Dr J.A. Smart, Marwood Hill Gardens, Marwood, Barnstaple, Devon, EX31 4EB

Bergenia
Chris Hallsworth, 27 The Promenade, Maylandsea, Essex CM3 6AR.
J. Roebuck, Cambridge City Parks, Propagation Centre, Cherry Hinton Park, Cherry Hinton Road, Cambridge, CB1 4DW
P. Orriss, Superintendent, University Botanic Garden, Bateman Street, Cambridge, CB2 lJF

Heuchera
Mary Ramsdale, 'Winkfield', Swan Hill Road, Colyford, Colyton, Devon, EX13 6QJ

Rodgersia
Heather Booker, The Gate House, Lee, Ilfracombe, Devon, EX34 8LR
Nori and Sandra Pope, Hadspen Garden, Hadspen House, Castle Cary, Somerset, BA5 7NG

Saxifraga
P. Orriss, Superintendent, University Botanic Garden, Bateman Street, Cambridge, CB2 lJF

References

Armitage, A.M. 1989. *Herbaceous Perennial Plants*. Athens, Georgia, Varsity Press.
Beckett, K. (ed.) 1993. *Encyclopaedia of Alpines*. Pershore, Worcs., Alpine Garden Society.
Bloom, A. 1991. *Hardy Perennials*. London, Batsford.
Clausen, R.R. & Ekstrom, N.H. 1989. *Perennials for American Gardens*. New York, Random House.
Huxley, A.J. (ed.) 1992. *The New Royal Horticultural Society. Dictionary of Gardening* London, Macmillan.
Jellito, L. & Schacht, W. 1990. (3rd ed. revised Schacht, W. & Fessler, A.). *Hardy Herbaceous Perennials*. Oregon, USA, Timber Press.
Köhlein, F. 1984. *Saxifrages and Related Genera*. London, Batsford.
Maubach, A. 1992. A Life for Perennials: Georg Arends *The Hardy Plant*, 14, 2.
Phillips, R. & Rix, M. 1991. Perennials. 2 vols. Londoon, Pan Books Ltd.
Thomas, G. S. 3rd ed. 1990. *Perennial Garden Plants* London, J.M. Dent & Sons
Thomas, G. S. 1970. *Plants for Ground Cover* London, J.M. Dent & Sons.
Webb, D.A. & Gornall, R.J. 1989. *Saxifrages of Europe*. London, Christopher Helm.

Glossary

Anther – the part of the stamen which contains the pollen.
Axil – the angle between the leaf stalk and the stem.
Biternate – a leaf that divides into three and then into three again.
Calyx – a collective term for the sepals, the outer parts of a flower, usually green.
Ciliate – with a fringe of hairs on the margin.
Clone – the vegetatively propagated progeny of a single plant, genetically identical to the parent.
Cordate – heart-shaped, with rounded lobes at the base.
Corymb – a racemose inflorescence in which lower flower stalks are longer than the upper so the flowers lie in a flattish dome; the outer flowers open first.
Crenate – with shallow, rounded teeth.

Cultivar – a cultivated variety having a particular name, expressed in single inverted commas e.g. 'Greenfinch'.

Denticulate – finely toothed.

Genus – a grouping of species.

Glaucous – having a whitish, blue-green or grey bloom, particularly on the leaves.

hort. – of the garden, of gardens or of gardeners. A name used in horticultural publications but not validly published according to the articles of the International Code of Botanical Nomenclature. Some such names are misapplied in gardens, though they may be validly used for a different plant.

Hybrid – the progeny of two genetically dissimilar parents.

Inflorescence – the arrangement of flowers and their accessory parts on a flowering shoot.

Node – the point on the stem of a plant where a leaf or bud grows.

Ovate – egg-shaped.

Palmate – with lobes or leaflets spread like the fingers of a hand.

Panicle – an inflorescence comprising several racemose parts; a compound raceme.

Peltate – shield-shaped, usually of a leaf. Having the petiole attached at or near the middle of the under surface.

Petiole – a leaf stalk.

Petiolule – a leaflet stalk.

Pinnate – a compound leaf having a series of leaflets arranged on each side of a common petiole, the leaflets usually opposite but sometimes alternate.

Pubescent – having a coating of short, fine, soft hairs.

Raceme – flowers spaced along a central stem with the ones at the base opening first.

Rhizome – a stem, often swollen and fleshy, subterranean or lying close to the soil surface that produces roots and aerial parts along its length.

Rootstock – the part of the plant from which the roots and the stems arise.

Scape – a long flower stalk rising directly from the root or rhizome.

Species – the basic unit of plant classification. A group of individuals which have common characteristics, distinct from other groups.

Sport – any freak, or somatic mutation, that deviates from the basic type, usually naturally.

Stolon – a branch or stem which comes into contact with the ground and may produce a new plant at soil level.

Variety (botanical variety or varietas) – a group of plants within a species, differing in minor characteristics and generally occurring naturally. Often confused with the term 'cultivar', which is used for cultivated varieties.